THE

# BIBLE AGAINST SLAVERY:

OR,

# AN INQUIRY

INTO THE

GENIUS OF THE MOSAIC SYSTEM, AND THE TEACHINGS
OF THE OLD TESTAMENT ON THE SUBJECT
OF HUMAN RIGHTS.

---

UNITED PRESBYTERIAN BOARD OF PUBLICATION.
PITTSBURGH.
1864.

Republished, 1970
Negro History Press – P. O. Box 5129 – Detroit, Michigan 48236

Standard Book Number 403-00185-4
Library of Congress Catalog Card Number: 74-92447

*113448*

This edition is printed on a high-quality,
acid-free paper that meets specification
requirements for fine book paper referred
to as "300-year" paper

# TO THE READER.

THE events of the last year—the President's Proclamation of Emancipation to Three Millions—the actual freeing of hundreds of thousands by the advance of our armies—the turning of sixty thousand slaves into soldiers—the rebellion grown desperate and raving in the frenzy that precedes collapse—these, with thick-coming events, already revealing the sole, sure basis of reconstruction, all combine to confront us anew with the question of slavery, its fundamental discussion and final adjustment; summoning all to such work for the hour as befits freemen and Christians.

To discharge, in part, their own responsibilities imposed by the crisis, the Board of Publication of the United Presbyterian Church reprint this work.

The argument was published twenty-seven years ago, in the *Anti-Slavery Quarterly Magazine.* It was afterward stereotyped and passed through four editions, the last in 1838. Soon after that the plates were destroyed, and for twenty years it has been out of print.

( iii )

When first published, many copies were sent through the post-office into the Slave States. Most of these were publicly burned at their places of delivery.

A copy that escaped the flames in Charleston, South Carolina, fell into the hands of Rev. Wm. H. Brisbane, a slaveholding Baptist clergyman and editor in that city. He sat down to confute the argument, but before his first number was ready for the types, he found that the faith he scouted had become his own. He left his native state, made his slaves free, settled them in Ohio, and published an able work, vindicating the Bible from pro-slavery perversions.

The present edition of this valuable work has been prepared for the press by the author, who has made some slight changes and abbreviations where such could be made without obscuring the sense, so that we are confident this edition will be found more perfect than any of its predecessors. In hopes that through the blessing of God it may exert some influence in freeing our beloved land from the blight of slavery, and ushering in that happy day now dawning when every yoke shall be broken, and the oppressed go free, we have concluded to issue the present edition.

PITTSBURG, PA., *January*, 1864.

# CONTENTS.

( v )

## OBJECTIONS CONSIDERED.

# THE BIBLE AGAINST SLAVERY.

SLAVERY seeks refuge in the Bible only in its last extremity. It seizes the horns of the altar in desperation, rushing from the terror of the avenger's arm. Like other unclean spirits, it "hateth the light, neither cometh to the light, lest its deeds should be reproved." Goaded to frenzy in its conflicts with conscience and common sense, denied all quarter, and hunted from every covert, it vaults at last into the sacred inclosure and courses up and down the Bible, "seeking rest, and finding none." THE LAW OF LOVE, glowing on every page, flashes through it anguish and despair. It shrinks from the hated light, and howls under the consuming touch, as demons recoiled from the Son of God, and shrieked, "Torment us not." At last, it slinks away under the types of the Mosaic system, and seeks to burrow out of sight among their shadows. Vain hope! Its asylum is its sepulchre; its city of refuge, the city of destruction. It flies from light into the sun; from heat into devouring fire; and from the voice of God into the thickest of His thunders.

2

## DEFINITION OF SLAVERY.

If we would know whether the Bible sanctions slavery, we must first determine *what slavery is.* An element is one thing ; a relation, another; an appendage, another. Relations and appendages presuppose other things to which they belong. To regard them as the things themselves, or as constituent parts of them, leads to endless confusion. Political disabilities are often confounded with slavery ; so are many relations and tenures indispensable to the social state. We will specify some of these.

1. PRIVATION OF SUFFRAGE. Then minors are slaves.

2. INELIGIBILITY TO OFFICE. Then females are slaves.

3. TAXATION WITHOUT REPRESENTATION. Then citizens in the District of Columbia are slaves.

4. PRIVATION OF ONE'S OATH IN LAW. Then in some States atheists are slaves.

5. PRIVATION OF TRIAL BY JURY. Then all in Russia are slaves.

6. BEING REQUIRED TO SUPPORT A PARTICULAR RELIGION. Then the people of England are slaves.

7. APPRENTICESHIP. The rights and duties of master and apprentice are correlative. The *claim* of each upon the other results from his *obligation* to the other. Apprenticeship is based on the principle of equivalent for value received. The rights of the apprentice are secured, equally with those of the master. Indeed, while the law is *just* to the latter, it is *benevolent* to

the former; its main design being rather to benefit the apprentice than the master. To the master it secures a mere compensation—to the apprentice a compensation and a virtual gratuity, he being the greater gainer. The law recognizes the *right* of the apprentice to a reward for his labor, prescribes the wages, and enforces the payment. The master's claim covers only the *services* of the apprentice. The apprentice's claim covers *equally* the services of the master. Neither can hold the other as property; but each holds property in the services of the other, and BOTH EQUALLY.

8. FILIAL SUBORDINATION AND PARENTAL CLAIMS. Both are nature's dictates, and elements of the social state; the natural affections which blend parent and child in one, excite each to discharge those offices incidental to the relation, and are a shield for mutual protection. The parent's legal claim to the child's services is a slight return for his care, toil, and outlays for support and education. This provision is, with the mass, indispensable to the family state. The child, in helping his parents, helps himself—increases a common stock, in which he has a share; while his services do but acknowledge a debt that money cannot cancel.

9. CLAIMS OF GOVERNMENTS ON SUBJECTS. Governments owe their subjects protection; subjects owe just governments allegiance and support. The obligations of both are reciprocal, and the benefits, mutual.

10. BONDAGE FOR CRIME. Must innocence be punished because guilt suffers penalties? True, the criminal works for the government without pay; and well he may. He owes the government. A century's work would not pay its drafts on him. He will die a public

defaulter. Because laws make men pay their debts, shall those be forced who owe nothing? The law makes no criminal, PROPERTY. It restrains his liberty, and makes him pay a fraction of his debt to the government; but it does not make him a chattel. Test it. To own property is to own its product. Are children, born of convicts, government property? Besides, can *property* be guilty? Can *chattels* deserve punishment?

11. RESTRAINTS UPON FREEDOM. Children are restrained by parents, pupils by teachers, patients by physicians, corporations by charters, and legislatures by constitutions. Embargoes, tariffs, quarantine, and all other laws keep men from doing as they please. Restraints are the web of civilized society, warp and woof. Are they slavery? then a government of LAW is the climax of slavery!

12. INVOLUNTARY OR COMPULSORY SERVICE. A juryman is empanelled against his will, and sit he *must*. A sheriff orders his posse; bystanders *must* turn in. Men are *compelled* to remove nuisances, pay fines and taxes, support their families, and "turn to the right as the law directs." Are they therefore slaves? To confound slavery with involuntary service is absurd. Slavery is a *condition*. The slave's *feelings* toward it cannot alter its nature. Whether he desire or detest it, the condition is the same. The slave's willingness to be a slave is no palliation of the slaveholder's guilt. Suppose he should believe himself a chattel, and consent to be treated as one, would that *make* him a chattel, or make those guiltless who *hold* him as such? I may be sick of life, and I tell

the assassin so that stabs me; is he any the less a murderer? Does my *consent* to his crime atone for it? my partnership in his guilt blot out his part of it? The slave's willingness to be a slave, so far from lessening the guilt of his "owner," aggravates it. If slavery has so palsied his mind that he looks upon himself as a chattel, and consents to be one, to hold him as such confirms his delusion, and reasserts the impious falsehood. Such feelings and convictions of the slave would increase tenfold the guilt of his master, in refusing to recognize him as a MAN, and thus to break the sorcery that cheats him out of his birthright—the consciousness of his worth and destiny.

Many of the foregoing conditions are *appendages* of slavery, but no one, nor all of them together, constitute its intrinsic element.

ENSLAVING MEN IS REDUCING THEM TO ARTICLES OF PROPERTY—making them chattels—converting *persons* into *things*—turning immortality into *merchandise*. A *slave* is one held in this condition. In law "he owns nothing, and can acquire nothing." His right to himself is abrogated. If he say *my* hands, *my* body, *my* mind, MY*self*, they are figures of speech. To *use himself* for his own good is a *crime*. To keep what he earns is *stealing*. To take his body into his own keeping is *insurrection*. In a word, the profit of his master is made the END of his being, and he, a *mere means* to that end—a mere means to an end into which his interests do not enter, of which they constitute ___tion. To deprive human nature of *any* of its ___*on*; to take away the *foundation* of In other words, whatever sinks

2*

man from an END to a mere *means,* just so far makes him a slave. MAN, sunk to a *thing!* the intrinsic element, the *principle* of slavery; MEN, bartered, leased, mortgaged, bequeathed, invoiced, shipped as cargoes, stored as goods, taken on executions, and knocked off at public outcry! Their *rights,* another's conveniences; their interests, wares on sale; their happiness, a household utensil; their personal ownership, a serviceable article or a plaything, as best suits the humor of the hour; their deathless nature, conscience, social affections, sympathies, hopes—marketable commodities! We repeat it, THE REDUCTION OF PERSONS TO THINGS! Not robbing a man of privileges, but of *himself;* not loading him with burdens, but making him a *beast of burden;* not restraining liberty, but subverting it; not curtailing rights, but abolishing them; not inflicting personal cruelty, but annihilating *personality;* not exacting involuntary labor, but sinking man into an *implement* of labor; not abridging human comforts, but abrogating human *nature.;* not depriving an animal of immunities, but despoiling a rational being of attributes—uncreating a MAN to make room for a *thing!*

That this is American slavery is shown by the laws of slave States. Judge Stroud, in his "Sketch of the Laws relating to Slavery," says, "The cardinal principle of slavery, that the slave is not to be ranked among sentient beings, but among *things,* obtains as undoubted law in all of these [the slave] States." The law of South Carolina says, "Slaves shall be deemed, held, taken, reputed, and adjudged in law to be chattels personal in the hands of their owners and possessors, and their executors, administrators, and assigns, to ALL INTENTS, CONSTRUCTIONS, AND PURPOSES WHATSOEVER."—*Brev. Dig.*, 229. In Louisiana, "A slave is one who is in the power of a master to whom he belongs; the master may sell him, dispose of his person, his industry, and his labor; he can do nothing, possess nothing, nor acquire anything, but what must belong to his master."—*Civ. Code*, Art. 35.

This is American slavery. The eternal distinction between a person and a thing, blotted out—the crowning distinction of all others—alike the source, the test, and the measure of their value—the rational, immortal principle, consecrated by God to universal homage in a baptism of glory and honor, by the gift of his Son, his Spirit, his Word, his presence, providence, and power; his shield, and staff, and sheltering wing; his opening heavens, and angels ministering, and chariots of fire, and songs of morning stars, and a great voice in heaven proclaiming eternal sanctions, and confirming the word with signs following.

Having stated the *principle* of American slavery, we ask, DOES THE BIBLE SANCTION SUCH A PRINCIPLE?* "To the *law* and the testimony!"

* The Bible record of actions is no comment on their moral character. It vouches for them as *facts*, not as *virtues*. It records without rebuke, Noah's drunkenness, Lot's incest, and the lies of Jacob and his mother—not only single acts, but *usages*, such as polygamy and concubinage, are entered on the record without censure. Is that *silent entry* God's *endorsement?* Because the Bible does not stamp on every crime its name and number, and write against it, *this is a crime*—does that wash out its guilt, and bleach it into a virtue?

## THE MORAL LAW AGAINST SLAVERY.

*Two* of the ten commandments deal death to slavery. "Thou shalt not steal," or, "Thou shalt not take from another what *belongs* to him." All a man's powers are God's gift to him. Each is a part of himself. All else that belongs to man is acquired by the *use* of these powers. The interest belongs to him, because the principal does; the product is his, because he is the producer. Ownership of anything is ownership of its *use*. The right to use according to will is *itself* ownership. The eighth commandment presupposes the right of every man to his powers, and their product. Slavery robs of both. A man's right to himself is his only absolute right—his right to anything else is *relative* to this, is derived from it, and held only by virtue of it. Self-right is the *foundation right*—the *post in the middle,* to which all other rights are fastened. Slaveholders, when asserting their right to their slaves, always assume their own right to themselves. The slaveholder knows it to be a self-evident proposition, that *a man belongs to himself*—that the right is intrinsic and absolute. In making out his own title, he makes out the title of every human being. As being *a man* is itself the title, all men have a common title deed. If one man's title is valid, all are valid. If one is worthless, all are. To deny the validity of the *slave's* title is to deny the validity of *his own;* and yet in making a man a slave, the slaveholder *asserts* the validity of his own title, while he seizes him as his property who has the *same* title to himself. Further, in making him a slave, he does not merely disfranchise of humanity *one* individual, but UNIVERSAL MAN. He destroys the foundations. He annihilates *all rights.* He attacks not only the human race, but all *rational being,* and rushes upon JEHOVAH. For rights are *rights ;* God's are no more—man's are no less.

The eighth commandment forbids the taking of *any part* of that which belongs to another. Slavery takes the *whole.* Does the Bible which prohibits the taking of *any* thing, sanction the taking of *every* thing? Does it thunder against the man who robs his neighbor of a *cent,* yet commission him to rob his neighbor of *himself?* Slaveholding is the highest possible violation of the eighth commandment. To take from a man his earnings, is theft. But to take the *earner* is a compound, life-long theft—supreme robbery that vaults up the climax at a leap—the dread, terrific, giant robbery, that towers among other robberies a solitary horror. The eighth commandment forbids the taking away, and the tenth adds, " Thou shalt not *covet* anything that is thy neighbor's ;" thus guarding every man's right to himself and his property, by making not only the actual taking away a sin, but even that state of mind which *tempts* to it. Who ever made human beings slaves, without *coveting* them? Why take their time, labor, liberty, right of self-improvement, their right to acquire property, to worship according to conscience, to search the Scriptures, to live with their families, and their right to their own bodies, if they do not *desire* them? They COVET them for purposes of gain, convenience, lust of domin-

ion, of sensual gratification, of pride and ostentation.
THEY BREAK THE TENTH COMMANDMENT, and pluck
down upon their heads the plagues that are written in
the book.   *Ten* commandments constitute the brief
compend of human duty.   *Two* of these brand slavery
as sin.

## MANSTEALING—EXAMINATION OF EX. XXI. 16.

The giving of the law at Sinai immediately pre-
ceded the promulgation of that body of laws called
the "Mosaic system."  Over the gateway of that
system, dread words were written by the finger of God
—"HE THAT STEALETH A MAN AND SELLETH HIM, OR
IF HE BE FOUND IN HIS HAND, HE SHALL SURELY BE
PUT TO DEATH."* Ex. xxi. 16.

The oppression of the Israelites in Egypt proclaims
the reason for such a law at such a time.  They had
just been emancipated.  The tragedies of their house
of bondage peopled their memories with thronging
horrors.  They had just witnessed God's testimony
against oppression in the plagues of Egypt—the
burning blains on man and beast; the dust quick-

* A writer in the American Quarterly Review, comment-
ing on this passage, thus blasphemes.  "On this passage an
impression has gone abroad that slave-owners are necessarily
menstealers; how hastily any one will perceive who consults
the passage in its connection.  Being found in the chapter
which authorizes this species of property among the Hebrews,
it must of course relate to *its full protection from the danger of
being enticed away from its rightful owner.*"—Am. Quart.
Review for June, 1833.   Article "Negro Slavery."

ened into loathsome life, and swarming upon every
living thing; the streets, the palaces, the temples,
and every house heaped up with the carcases of
things abhorred; the kneading troughs and ovens, the
secret chambers and the couches, reeking and dissolv-
ing with the putrid death; the pestilence walking in
darkness at noonday, the devouring locusts, and hail
mingled with fire, the first-born death-struck, and the
waters blood; and last of all, that dread high hand
that whelmed the monarch and his hosts, and strewed
their corpses on the sea. All this their eyes had
looked upon; earth's proudest city, wasted and
thunder-scarred, lying in desolation, and the doom of
oppressors traced on her ruins in the hand-writing of
God, glaring in letters of fire mingled with blood—a
blackened monument of wrath to the utmost against
the stealers of men. No wonder that God, in a code
of laws prepared for such a people at such a time,
should uprear on its foreground a blazing beacon to
flash terror on slaveholders. *"He that stealeth a
man and selleth him, or if he be found in his hand,
he shall surely be put to death."* Ex. xxi. 16. Deut.
xxiv. 7.\* God's cherubim and flaming sword guarding the entrance to the Mosaic system!

\* Jarchi, who wrote seven hundred years ago, and was the
most eminent of the Jewish Commentators, in his comment
on this stealing and making merchandise of men, gives the
meaning, thus: "Using a man against his will, as a servant
lawfully purchased; yea, though he should use his services
ever so little, only to the value of a farthing, or use but his
arm to lean on to support him, *if he be forced so to act as a
servant*, the person compelling him but once to do so, shall die
as a thief, whether he has sold him or not."

The word *Gănăbh* here rendered *stealeth*, means, the taking of what belongs to another, whether by violence or fraud; the same word is used in the eighth commandment, and prohibits both robbery and theft.

The crime specified is that of depriving SOMEBODY of the ownership of a man. Is this somebody a master? and is the crime that of depriving a master of his servant? Then it would have been "he that stealeth" a *servant*, not "he that stealeth a *man*." If the crime had been the taking of an individual from *another*, then the *term* used would have been expressive of that relation, and most especially if it was the relation of property to a *proprietor!*

The crime is stated in a threefold form—man *stealing*, *selling*, and *holding*. All are put on a level, and whelmed under one penalty—DEATH.* This *somebody* deprived of the ownership of a man, is the *man himself*, robbed of personal ownership. Joseph said, "Indeed I was *stolen* away out of the land of the Hebrews." Gen. xl. 15. How *stolen?* His brethren sold him as an article of merchandise. Contrast this penalty for *man*-stealing with that for *property*-stealing, Ex. xxii. 1, 4. If a man had stolen an *ox* and killed or sold it, he was to restore five oxen; if he had neither sold nor killed it, two oxen. But in the case of stealing a *man*, the *first* act drew down the utmost power of punishment. The fact that the penalty for *man*-stealing was death, and the penalty for *property*-stealing the mere restoration of double, shows that the

---

* "Those are *men-stealers* who abduct, *keep*, sell, or buy slaves or freemen."—GROTIUS.

two cases were adjudicated on opposite principles.
The man stolen might be diseased or past labor; consequently, instead of being profitable to the thief, he
would be a tax; yet death was still the penalty, though
not a cent's worth of *property-value* was taken. The
penalty for stealing property was a mere property-
penalty. However large the theft, the payment of
double wiped out the score. It might have a greater
money value than a thousand men, yet death was not
the penalty, nor even stripes, but double *of the same
kind*. Why was not the rule uniform? When a *man*
was stolen, why was not the thief required to restore
double of the same kind—two men, or if he had sold
him, five men? Do you say that the man-thief might
not *have* them? So the ox-thief might not have two
oxen, or if he had killed it, five. But if God permitted
men to hold *men* as property, as well as oxen, the
man-thief could get men with whom to pay the
penalty, as well as the ox-thief oxen. Further, when
property was stolen, the legal penalty was a compensation to the person injured. But when a *man* was
stolen, no property compensation was offered. To
tender money would have been to repeat the outrage
with intolerable aggravations. Compute the value
of a MAN in *money!* Throw dust into the scale
against immortality! The law recoiled against such
supreme insult and impiety. To have permitted the
man-thief to expiate his crime by restoring double
would have been making the repetition of crime its
atonement. But the infliction of death for man-steal-
ing exacted the utmost possibility of reparation. It
wrung from the guilty wretch as he gave up the ghost,

3

a testimony in death-groans, to the infinite dignity of man—a proclamation to the universe, voiced in mortal agony, " MAN IS INVIOLABLE !"—a confession shrieked at the grave's mouth—" I die accursed, and God is just !".

If God permitted man to hold man as property, why did he punish for stealing that kind of property infinitely more than for stealing any other kind of property ? Why punish with death for stealing a very little of *that* sort of property, and make a mere fine the penalty for stealing a thousand times as much of any other property—especially if, by his own act, God had annihilated the difference between man and *property*, by putting him on a level with it ?

The guilt of a crime depends much upon the nature and condition of the victim. To steal is a crime, whoever the thief, or whatever the plunder. To steal bread from a full man is theft; to steal it from a starving man is both theft and murder. If I steal my neighbor's property, the crime consists not in altering the *nature* of the article, but in taking as *mine* what is *his*. But when I take my neighbor himself, and first make him *property*, and then *my* property, the latter act, which was the sole crime in the former case, dwindles to nothing. The sin in stealing a man is not the transfer from its owner to another of that which is property, but the turning of *personality* into *property*. The attributes of man remain, but the rights and immunities which grow out of them are annihilated. It is the first law of reason to regard things and beings as they are ; and the sum of religion, to feel and act toward them according to their value.

Knowingly to treat them otherwise is sin; and the degree of violence done to their nature, relations, and value, measures its guilt. When things are sundered which God has indissolubly joined, or confounded in one, which he has separated by infinite extremes; when sacred and eternal distinctions are derided and set at nought, then sin reddens to its "scarlet dye." The sin specified is that of doing violence to the *nature* of a *man.* In the verse preceding, and in that which follows, the same principle is laid down. Verse 15, "He that smiteth his father or his mother shall surely be put to death." Verse 17, "He that curses his father or his mother shall surely by put to death." If a Jew smote his neighbor, the law smote him in return; but if the blow were given to a *parent,* the law struck the smiter dead. The parental relation is the *centre* of human society. To violate that, is to violate all. Whoever tramples on that, shows that *no* relation has any sacredness in his eyes—that he is unfit to move among human relations who violates one so sacred and tender. Therefore the Mosaic law uplifted his corpse, and brandished the ghastly terror around the parental relation to guard it from inroad.

Why is there such a difference in penalties, for the same act? Answer. 1. The relation violated was obvious—the distinction self-evident, dictated by a law of nature. 2. The act was a violence done to constitutional susceptibilities. 3. The parental relation is the focal point of the social system. "*Honor thy father and thy mother,*" stands at the head of those commands which prescribe the duties of man to man. In this case, death was to be inflicted not for smiting a *man,*

but a *parent.* In the next verse, " He that stealeth
a man," &c., the SAME PRINCIPLE is wrought out in
still stronger relief. The crime to be punished with
death was not the taking of property from its owner,
but violence to an *immortal nature,* the blotting out
a sacred *distinction*—making MEN " chattels."

With incessant pains the Bible exalts the distinction
between persons and things. " In the beginning" God
proclaimed it to the universe as it rose into being. Crea-
tion stood up at the instant of its birth to do it homage.
It paused in adoration while God ushered forth its
crowning work. Why that dread pause and that crea-
ting arm held back in mid career, and that high con-
ference in the godhead ? " Let us make man in OUR
IMAGE, after OUR LIKENESS, and let him have dominion
over the fish of the sea, and over the fowl of the air,
and over the cattle, and over all the earth." Then,
while every living thing, with land, and sea, and firma-
ment, and marshalled worlds, waited to swell the shout
of morning stars—then " God created man IN HIS OWN
IMAGE ; IN THE IMAGE OF GOD created he him." This
solves the problem, IN THE IMAGE OF GOD
CREATED HE HIM. This distinction is often
repeated. In Gen. i. 26–28, it is expressed in various
forms. In Gen. v. 1, we find it again, " IN THE LIKE-
NESS OF GOD MADE HE HIM." In Gen. ix. 6, again.
After giving license to shed the blood of " every mov-
ing thing that liveth," it is added, " *Whoso sheddeth
man's blood, by man shall his blood be shed, for* IN
THE IMAGE OF GOD MADE HE MAN." As though it
had been said, " All these creatures are your property,
designed for your use—they have the likeness of earth,

their spirits go downward; but MAN has my own likeness : IN THE IMAGE OF GOD made I man ; an intelli-
gent, immortal agent, invited to all that I can give
and he can be. So in Lev. xxiv. 17, 18, 21, "He
that killeth any MAN shall surely be put to death; and
he that killeth a beast shall make it good, beast for
beast ; and he that killeth a man, he shall be put to
death." So in Ps. viii. 5, 6, is an enumeration of
particulars, each separating infinitely MEN from
brutes and things ! 1. " *Thou hast made him a little
lower than the angels.*" Slavery drags him down
among *brutes.* 2. "*And hast crowned him with
glory and honor.*" Slavery tears off his crown, and
puts on a *yoke.* 3. " *Thou madest him to have
dominion** OVER *the works of thy hands.*" Slavery
breaks his sceptre, and casts him down *among* those

---

* In Gen. i. 28, God says to man, "*Have dominion* over the
fish of the sea, and over the fowl of the air and over every
living thing that moveth upon the earth," thus vesting in
*every* human being the right of ownership over the earth, its
products and animal life, and in *each* human being the *same*
right. By so doing God prohibited the exercise of ownership
by man over *man;* for the grant to *all* men of *equal* ownership, forestalled the exercise of ownership over *each other*, as
whoever is the owner of a *man*, is the owner of his *right of
property*—in other words, when one man becomes the property of another his *rights* become such too, his *right of property* is transferred to his " owner," and thus as far as *himself* is concerned, is annihilated. Finally, by originally
investing *all* men with dominion or ownership over property,
God proclaimed the *right of all* to exercise it, and pronounced
every man who takes it away a robber of the highest grade.
Such is every slaveholder.

3*

works—yea, *beneath them.* 4. " *Thou hast put all things under his feet.*" Slavery puts HIM under the feet of an " owner." Who, but an impious scorner, dare thus mutilate the IMAGE of his Maker, and blaspheme the Holy One, who saith, " *Inasmuch as ye did it unto one of the least of these, ye did it unto* ME ?"

In prosecuting this inquiry, the Patriarchal and Mosaic systems will be considered together, as each reflects light upon the other, and as many regulations of the latter are mere *legal* forms of institutions previously existing. Whatever were the usages of the patriarchs, God has not made them our exemplars.* The question to be settled by us is not what were Jewish *customs*, but what were the rules that God gave for their regulation.

Before analyzing the condition of servants under these two states of society, we will consider the import of certain terms which describe the mode of procuring them.

---

* Those who insist that the patriarchs held slaves, and sit with such delight under their shadow, hymning the praises of "those good old slaveholders and patriarchs," might at small cost greatly augment their numbers. A single stanza celebrating patriarchal *concubinage*, winding off with a chorus in honor of patriarchal *drunkenness*, would be a trumpet-call, summoning from brothel, bush, and brake, highway and hedge, and sheltering fence, a brotherhood of kindred affinities, each claiming Abraham or Noah as his patron saint!

## IMPORT OF "BUY," AND "BOUGHT WITH MONEY."

As the Israelites were commanded to "buy" their servants, and as Abraham had servants "bought with money," it is argued that servants were articles of property! The sole ground for this belief is *the terms themselves!* What a gain, if, in discussion, the thing to be proved were always *assumed!* To beg the question in debate saves the trouble of proving it. Instead of investigation into Scripture usage to settle the meaning of terms, let every man interpret the oldest book in the world by the usages of his own time and place, and the work is done! Every man would have an infallible clue to the mind of the Spirit, in the dialect of his own neighborhood! Suppose we take it for granted that the sense in which words are *now* used is the *inspired* sense. David says, " I prevented the dawning of the morning, and cried." What, stop the earth in its revolution! Two hundred years ago, *prevent* was used in its strict Latin sense, to *come before,* or *anticipate.* David's expression, in the English of the nineteenth century, would be, " Before the dawning of the morning, I cried." In the Bible, many words are used in a sense now nearly, or quite obsolete, and sometimes in a sense totally *opposite* to their present meaning. A few examples follow : " I purposed to come to you, but was *let* (hindered) hitherto."—"And the four *beasts* (living ones) fell down, and worshipped God."— " Whosoever shall *offend* (cause to sin) one of these little ones."—" Go out into the highways, and *compel*

(urge) them to come in."—"Only let your *conversa-tion* (habitual conduct) be as becometh the Gospel."
—"The Lord Jesus Christ who shall judge the *quick* (living) and the dead."—"They that seek me *early* (earnestly) shall find me."—"So when tribulation or persecution ariseth *by and by* (immediately), they are offended." Nothing is more mutable than language. Words, like bodies, are always throwing off particles, and absorbing others. So long as they are mere representatives, elected by universal suffrage, their meaning will be a perfect volatile, and to cork it up, expecting to keep it from evaporation for centuries, is an employment sufficiently silly for slaveholding doctors of divinity. Was there ever a shallower conceit than that of establishing the sense attached to a word centuries ago, by showing what it means *now?* Pity that fashionable mantuamakers were not a little quicker at taking hints from some Doctors of Divinity! How easily they might save their pious customers all qualms of conscience about fashionable exposures, by proving that the last importation of Parisian indecency, now showing off on promenade, was the very style of dress in which the modest Sarah kneaded cakes for the angels!

The inference, that the word buy, used to describe the procuring of servants, means procuring them as *chattels,* assumes that whatever *costs* money *is* money ; that whatever or whoever you pay money *for,* is an article of property, and the fact of your paying for it *proves* it property. 1. The children of Israel were required to purchase their first-born from under the obligations of the priesthood, Num. xviii. 15, 16 ; iii.

45–51; Ex. xiii. 13; xxxiv. 20. This custom still exists among the Jews, and the word *buy* is still used to describe the transaction. Does this prove that their first-born were, or are held as property? They were *bought* as really as were *servants*. 2. The Israelites were required to pay money for their own souls. This is called sometimes a ransom, sometimes an atonement. Were their souls therefore marketable commodities? 3. When the Israelites set apart themselves or their children to the Lord by vow, for the performance of some service, an express statute provided that a *price* should be set upon the "*persons*," and it prescribed the manner and *terms* of the "estimation" or valuation, by the payment of which the persons might be *bought off* from the service vowed. The *price* for males from one month old to five years was five shekels, for females three; from five years old to twenty, for males, twenty shekels, for females ten; from twenty years old to sixty, for males, fifty shekels, for females thirty; about sixty years old, for males, fifteen shekels, for females ten. Lev. xxvii. 2–8. Were these descriptions of persons goods and chattels, because they were *bought*, and their *prices* regulated by law? 4.. Bible saints *bought* their wives. Boaz bought Ruth. "Moreover, Ruth, the Moabitess, the wife of Mahlon, have I *purchased* (bought) to be my wife." Ruth iv. 10.*

---

* In the verse preceding, Boaz says, "I have *bought* all that was Elimelech's * * * of the hand of Naomi." In the original, the same word (kānā) is used in both verses. In the 9th, "a parcel of land" is "bought," in the 10th a

Hosea bought his wife. "So I *bought* her to me for fifteen pieces of silver, and for a homer of barley, and an half homer of barley." Hosea iii. 2. Jacob bought his wives, Rachel and Leah, and paid for them in labor. Gen. xxix. 15–23. Moses probably bought his wife in the same way, as the servant of her father.* Exod. ii. 21. Shechem, when negotiating with Jacob and his sons for Dinah, says, "Ask me never so much dowry and gift, and I will give according as ye shall say unto me." Gen. xxxiv. 11, 12. David purchased Michal, and Othniel Achsah, by performing perilous services for the fathers of the damsels. 1 Sam. xviii. 25–27; Judg. i. 12, 13. That the purchase of wives, either with money or by services, was the general practice, is plain from such passages as Ex. xxii. 17, and 1 Sam. xviii. 25. Among the modern Jews this usage exists, though now a mere form. Yet among their marriage ceremonies is one called "marrying by the penny." The similarity in the methods of procuring wives and servants, in the terms employed in describing the transactions, and in the prices paid for each is worthy of

---

"wife" is "bought." If the Israelites had been as profound at inferences as our modern commentators, they would have put such a fact as this to the rack till they had tortured out of it a divine warrant for holding their wives as property and speculating in the article whenever it happened to be scarce.

* This custom still prevails in some eastern countries. The Crim Tartars, when poor, serve an apprenticeship for their wives, during which they live under the same roof with them, and at the close of it are adopted into the family.

notice. The highest price of wives (virgins) and servants was the same. Comp. Deut. xxii. 28, 29, and Ex. xxii. 17, with Lev. xxvii. 2–8. The *medium* price of wives and servants was the same. Comp. Hos. iii. 2, with Ex. xxi. 32. Hosea seems to have paid one-half in money and the other half in grain. Further, the Israelitish female bought-servants were *wives*, their husbands and masters being the same persons. Ex. xxi. 8, Judg. xix. 3, 27. If *buying* servants proves them property, buying wives proves *them* property. Why not contend that the *wives* of the ancient fathers of the faithful were their " chattels," and used as ready change at a pinch ; and thence deduce the rights of modern husbands ?

This use of the word buy is not peculiar to the Hebrew. In the Syriac, the common expression for "the espoused" is "the bought." Even so late as the 16th century, the common record of *marriages* in the old German Chronicles was, " A BOUGHT B."

The word translated *buy* is like other words, modified by the nature of the subject to which it is applied. Eve said, " I have *gotten* (bought) a man from the Lord." She named him Cain, that is, *bought.* " He that heareth reproof, getteth (buyeth) understanding." Prov. xv. 32. So in Isa. xi. 11. " The Lord shall set his hand again to recover (to *buy*) the remnant of his people." So Ps. lxxviii. 54. " He brought them to his mountain which his right hand had *purchased*," (gotten.) Neh. v. 8. "We of our ability have *redeemed* (bought) our brethren the Jews, that were sold unto the heathen." Here " *bought*" is not applied to persons reduced to servitude, but to those

taken *out* of it.   Prov. viii. 22.   "The Lord possessed
(bought) me in the beginning of his way."   Prov.
xix. 8.   "He that *getteth* (buyeth) wisdom loveth his
own soul."   Finally, to *buy* is a *secondary* meaning
of the Hebrew word *kānā*.

Even at this day, the word *buy* is used to describe
the procuring of servants, where slavery is abolished.
In the British West Indies, where slaves became
apprentices in 1834, they are still (1837) "bought."
This is the current word in West India newspapers.
Ten years since servants were "*bought*" in New York,
and still are in New Jersey, as really as in Virginia,
yet the different senses in which the word is used in
these States put no man in a quandary.   Under the
system of legal *indenture* in Illinois, servants now are
"*bought*."*   Until   recently,   immigrants   to   this
country were "bought" in great numbers.   By voluntary contract they engaged to work a given time to
pay for their passage.   This class of persons, called
"redemptioners," consisted at one time of thousands.
Multitudes are "bought" *out* of slavery by themselves
or others.   Under the same roof with the writer is a
"servant bought with money."   A few weeks since,
she was a slave ; when "bought," she was a slave no
longer.   Alas ! for venal politicians, if "buying" men
makes them "chattels."   The histories of the revolu-

---

* The following statute is now in force in the free State of
Illinois : "No negro, mulatto, or Indian, shall at any time
*purchase* any servant other than of their own complexion ;
and if any of the persons aforesaid shall presume to *purchase*
a white servant, such servant shall immediately become free,
and shall be so held, deemed and taken."

tion tell us that Benedict Arnold was "bought" by
British gold, and that Williams, Pauldings, and Van
Wert could not be "bought" by Major André.
When a northern clergyman marries a rich southern
widow, country gossip thus hits it off, "The cotton
bags *bought* him." Sir Robert Walpole said, "Every
man has his price, and whoever will pay it can *buy*
him;" and John Randolph said, "The northern dele-
gation is in the market; give me money enough, and
I can *buy* them." Yet we have no floating visions of
"chattels personal," man-auctions, or coffles.

In Connecticut, town-paupers are "bought" by
those who become responsible to the town for their
support. If these "bought" persons labor for those
who "buy" them, it is wholly *voluntary.* They are
in no sense the "property" of their purchasers.*

The transaction between Joseph and the Egyptians
gives a clue to the use of "buy" and "bought with
money." Gen. xlvii. 18–26. The Egyptians proposed to Joseph to become servants. "Buy us," said
they. When the bargain was closed, Joseph said,

---

* The "select-men" of each town annually give notice,
that they will *sell* the poor of said town. The persons thus
"sold" are "bought" by such persons, approved by the
"select-men," as engage to furnish them with sufficient food,
clothing, medicine, &c., for such a sum as the parties may
agree upon. The Connecticut papers frequently contain
advertisements like the following :—

"NOTICE—The poor of the town of Chatham will be SOLD
on the first Monday in April, 1837, at the house of F. Penfield,
Esq., at 9 o'clock in the forenoon."—*Middletown Sentinel*,
Feb. 3, 1837.

4

"Behold, I have *bought* you this day." Neither party
regarded the persons *bought* as property, but as bound
to labor on certain conditions, to pay for their support during the famine.   This buying of *services* (in
this case it was but one-fifth part) is called in Scripture usage, *buying the persons*.   This case claims
special notice, as it is the only one where the whole
transaction of buying servants is detailed—the pre-
liminaries, the process, the mutual acquiescence, and
the permanent relation resulting therefrom.   In all
other instances, the fact is stated without particulars.
In this, the whole process is laid open.   1. The
persons "bought" *sold themselves,* and of their own
accord.   2. Paying for the permanent *service* of persons, or even a portion of it, is called "buying" those
persons ; just as paying for the *use* of land or houses
for a number of years is called in Scripture usage,
*buying* them.   See Lev. xxv. 28, 33, and xxvii. 24.
The objector takes it for granted that servants were
bought of *third* persons ; and thence infers that they
were articles of property.   Both are sheer *assump-
tions.*   No instance is recorded, under the Mosaic
system, in which a *master sold his servant.*

That servants who were "bought" *sold themselves*
is a fair inference from various passages of Scripture.*

---

* Those who insist that the servants which the Israelites
were commanded to buy of "the heathen which were round
about," were to be bought of *third persons*, charge God with
the inconsistency of affirming the right of those persons to
freedom, upon whom, say they, he pronounced the doom of
slavery.   For they tell us that the sentence of death uttered
against those heathen was commuted into slavery.   Now if

In Leviticus xxv. 47, the case of the Israelite, who became the servant of the stranger, the words are, "If he SELL HIMSELF unto the stranger." Yet the 51st verse informs us that this servant was " BOUGHT," and that the price of his purchase was paid to *himself.* The *same word*, and the same *form* of the word, which, in verse 47, is rendered *sell himself*, is, in verse 39 of the same chapter, rendered *be sold;* in Deut. xxviii. 68, the same word is rendered "be sold." "And there ye shall BE SOLD unto your enemies for bond-men and bond-women, and NO MAN SHALL BUY YOU." How could they "*be sold*" without *being bought*? Our translation makes it nonsense. The word *Mākar* rendered " *be sold*" is used here in the Hithpael conjugation, which is generally reflexive in

---

"the heathen round about" were doomed to slavery, the *sellers* were doomed as well as the *sold.* Where did the sellers get their right to sell? God, by commanding the Israelites to BUY, affirmed the right of *somebody* to *sell*, and that the *ownership* of what was sold existed. *somewhere;* which *right* and ownership he commanded them to *recognize.* Where then did the heathen *sellers* get their right to. sell, since *they* were doomed to slavery equally with those whom they sold? Did God's decree vest in them a right to *others* while it annulled their right to *themselves?* If one part of "the heathen round about" were *already* held as slaves by the other part, *such* of course were not *doomed* to slavery, for they were already slaves. So also, if those heathen who held them as slaves had a *right* to hold them, which right God commanded the Israelites to *buy out*, surely these *slave-holders* were not doomed by God to be slaves ; for, according to the objector, God had himself affirmed their right *to hold others as slaves*, and commanded his people to respect it.

its force, and, like the middle voice in Greek, represents what an individual does for himself, and should
manifestly have been rendered, "Ye shall *offer yourselves* for sale, and there shall be no purchaser."
For a clue to Scripture usage on this point, see 1
Kings xxi. 20, 25 : "Thou hast *sold thyself* to work
evil." "There was none like unto Ahab, which did
sell *himself* to work wickedness." 2 Kings xvii. 17 :
"They used divination and enchantments, and *sold
themselves* to do evil." Isa. l. 1 : "For your iniqui-
ties have ye *sold yourselves*." Isa. lii. 3 : "Ye
have *sold yourselves* FOR NOUGHT, and ye shall be
redeemed without money." See also, Jer. xxxiv.
14 ; Rom. vii. 14, vi. 16 ; John, viii. 34, and the
case of Joseph and the Egyptians, already quoted.
In the purchase of wives, it is generally stated that
they were bought of *third* persons. If *servants* were
bought of third persons, it is strange that no *instance*
of it is on record.

Let us now inquire into the *condition* of servants
under the patriarchal and Mosaic systems.


### 1. THE RIGHTS AND PRIVILEGES OF SERVANTS.

The design of the laws defining the relations of
master and servant was the good of both parties—
more especially that of the *servants*. While the
master's interests were guarded from injury, those of
the servants were *promoted*. These laws made a
merciful provision for the poorer classes, both of the
Israelites and strangers, not laying on burdens, but
lifting them—they were a grant of *privileges*.

I. BUYING SERVANTS WAS REGARDED AS A KINDNESS TO THE PERSONS BOUGHT, and as establishing between them and their purchasers a bond of affection and confidence. This is plain from the frequent use of the custom to illustrate the love and care of God for his people. Deut. xxxii. 6; Ex. xv. 16; Ps. lxxiv. 2; Prov. viii. 22.

II. NO STRANGER COULD JOIN THE FAMILY OF AN ISRAELITE WITHOUT BECOMING A PROSELYTE. Compliance with this condition was the *price of the privilege.* Gen. xvii. 9–14, 23, 27. In other words, to become a servant was virtually to become an Israelite.* Was then the relation of a proselyted servant to his master a sentence consigning to *punishment*, or a ticket of admission to *privileges?*

III. EXPULSION FROM THE FAMILY WAS THE DEPRIVATION OF A PRIVILEGE, IF NOT A PUNISHMENT. When Sarah took umbrage at the conduct of Hagar and Ishmael, " She said unto Abraham, *Cast out* this bond-woman and her son." * * And " Abraham

---

* The rites by which a stranger became a proselyte transformed him into a Jew. Compare 1 Chron. ii. 17, with 2 Sam. xvii. 25. In Esther viii. 17, it is said "Many of the people of the land *became Jews.*" In the Septuagint, the passage is thus rendered, "Many of the heathen were circumcised and became Jews." The incorporation of the proselytes with the Hebrews is shown by such passages as Isa. lvi. 6, 7, 8; Eph. ii. 11, 22; Num. x. 29–32. Calmet, Art. Proselyte, says, "They were admitted to all the prerogatives of the people of the Lord." Mohommed doubtless borrowed from the laws and usages of the Jews, his well known regulation for admitting proselytes to all civil and religious privileges.

4*

took bread and a bottle of water, and gave it unto Hagar and the child, and *sent her away.*" Gen. xxi. 10, 14. In Luke xvi. 1–8, our Lord tells us of the steward or head servant of a rich man who defrauded his master, and was excluded from his household. The servant, anticipating such a punishment, says, " I am resolved what to do, that when I am *put out* of the stewardship, they may receive me into their houses." The case of Gehazi appears to be similar. He was guilty of fraud and of deliberate lying, on account of which Elisha seems to have discarded him. 2 Kings v. 20–27. If a servant neglected any ceremonial rite, and was on that account excommunicated from the congregation of Israel, it excluded him also from the *family* of an Israelite. In other words, he could be a *servant* no longer than he was an *Israelite.* To forfeit the latter *distinction* involved the forfeiture of the former *privilege.*

IV. THE HEBREW SERVANT COULD COMPEL HIS MASTER TO KEEP HIM. When the six years' contract had expired, if the servant *demanded* it, the law *obliged* the master to retain him permanently, however little he might need his services. Deut. xv. 12–17; Ex. xxi. 2–6. This shows that the system was framed to advance the interests of the servant.

V. SERVANTS WERE ADMITTED INTO COVENANT WITH GOD. Deut. xxix. 10–13.

VI. THEY WERE GUESTS AT ALL NATIONAL AND FAMILY FESTIVALS. Ex. xii. 43–44; Deut. xii. 12, 18, xvi. 10–16.

VII. THEY WERE STATEDLY INSTRUCTED IN MORALITY AND RELIGION. Deut. xxxi. 10–13; Josh. viii. 33

–35 ; 2 Chron. xvii. 8–9, xxxv. 3, and xxxiv. 30 ;
Neh. viii. 7, 8.

VIII. THEY WERE RELEASED FROM THEIR REGULAR
LABOR NEARLY ONE-HALF OF THE WHOLE TIME. During which they had their support, and the same instruction that was provided for the other members of the
Hebrew community. The law secured to them—

1. *Every seventh year ;* Lev. xxv. 3–6 ; thus giving
to those who were servants during the entire period
between the jubilees, *eight whole years* (including the
jubilee year) of rest.

2. *Every seventh day.* This in forty-two years,
the eighth being subtracted from the fifty, would
amount to just *six years.*

3. *The three annual festivals.* Ex. xxiii. 17 ;
xxxiv. 23. The *Passover*, which commenced on the
15th of the 1st month, and lasted seven days, Deut.
xvi. 3, 8. The Pentecost, or Feast of Weeks, which
began on the 6th of the 3d month, and lasted seven
days. Deut. xvi. 10, 11. The Feast of Tabernacles, which commenced on the 15th of the 7th
month, and lasted eight days. Deut. xvi. 13, 15 ;
Lev. xxiii. 34–39. As all met in one place, much
time would be spent on the journey. Cumbered caravans move slowly. After their arrival, a day or two
would be requisite for divers preparations before the
celebration, besides some time at the close of it, in
preparations for return. If we assign three weeks to
each festival—including the time spent on the journeys, and the delays before and after the celebration,
together with the *festival week*, it will be a small
allowance for the cessation of their regular labor. As

there were three festivals in the year, the main body
of the servants would be absent from their stated employments at least *nine weeks annually*, which would
amount in forty-two years, subtracting the Sabbaths,
to six years and eighty-four days.

4. *The new moons.* The Jewish year had twelve ;
Josephus says that the Jews always kept *two* days for
the new moon. See Calmet on the Jewish Calendar,
and Horne's Introduction ; also 1 Sam. xx. 18, 19,
27. This, in forty-two years, would be two years 280
days.

5. *The feast of trumpets.* On the first day of the
seventh month, and of the civil year. Lev. xxiii. 24,
25.

6. *The atonement day.* On the tenth of the seventh
month. Lev. xxiii. 27.

These two feasts would consume not less than sixty-
five days not reckoned above.

Thus it appears that those who continued servants
during the period between the jubilees were by law
released from their labor, TWENTY-THREE YEARS AND
SIXTY-FOUR DAYS OUT OF FIFTY YEARS. In this calculation we have left out those numerous *local* festivals
to which frequent allusion is made, Judg. xxi. 19 ;
1 Sam. ix. 12, 22, etc., and the various *family* festivals, such as at the weaning of children ; at marriages ;
at sheep shearings ; at circumcisions ; at the making
of covenants, &c., to which reference is often made, as
in 1 Sam. xx. 6, 28, 29. Neither have we included
the festivals instituted at a later period—the feast of
Purim, Esth. ix. 28, 29 ; and of the Dedication, which
lasted eight days. John x. 22 ; 1 Mac. iv. 59.

Finally, the Mosaic system secured to servants an amount of time which, if distributed, would be almost ONE-HALF OF THE DAYS IN EACH YEAR. Meanwhile, they were supported, and furnished with opportunities of instruction.

The service of *national* servants or tributaries was regulated upon the same benevolent principle, and secured to them TWO-THIRDS of the whole year. "A month they were in Lebanon, and two months they were at home." 1 Kings, v. 13–15. Compared with 2 Chron. 11, 17–19, viii. 7–2; 1 Kings, ix. 20, 22. The regulations for the inhabitants of Gibeon, Chephirah, Beeroth and Kirjah-jearim (afterwards called *Nethinims*), must have secured to them nearly the whole of their time. If, as is probable, they served in courses corresponding to those of the priests whom they assisted, they were in actual service less than one month annually.

IX. THE SERVANT WAS PROTECTED BY THE LAW EQUALLY WITH THE OTHER MEMBERS OF THE COMMUNITY.

Proof.—"Judge righteously between every man and his brother, and THE STRANGER THAT IS WITH HIM." "Ye shall not RESPECT PERSONS in judgment, but ye shall hear the SMALL as well as the great." Deut. i. 16, 19. Also Lev. xix, 15; xxiv. 22. "Ye shall have one manner of law as well for the STRANGER, as for one of your own country." So Num. xv. 29. "Ye shall have ONE LAW for him that sinneth through ignorance, both for him that is born among the children of Israel and for the STRANGER that sojourneth among them." Deut. xxvii. 19. "Cursed be he that PER-

VERTETH THE JUDGMENT OF THE STRANGER."* Deut. xxvii. 19.

X. The Mosaic system enjoined affection and kindness towards servants, foreign as well as Jewish.

"The stranger that dwelleth with you shall be unto you as one born among you, and thou shalt love him as thyself.' Lev. xix. 34. "For the Lord your God * * REGARDETH NOT PERSONS. He doth execute the judgment of the fatherless and widow, and LOVETH THE STRANGER, in giving him food and raiment: LOVE YE THEREFORE THE STRANGER." Deut. x. 17, 19. "Thou shalt neither vex a STRANGER nor oppress him." Ex. xxii. 21. "Thou shalt not oppress a STRANGER, for ye know the heart of a stranger." Ex. xxiii. 9. "If thy brother be waxen poor, thou shalt relieve him, yea, though he be a STRANGER or sojourner, that he may live with thee: take thou no usury of him or increase, but fear thy God." Lev. xxv. 35, 36.

---

* In a work entitled, "Instruction in the Mosaic Religion," by Professor Jholson, of the Jewish Seminary at Frankfort-on-the-Main, translated into English by Rabbi Leeser, we find the following.—Sec. 165.

"Question. Does holy writ anywhere make a difference between the Israelite and the other who is no Israelite, in those laws and prohibitions which forbid us the *committal of anything against our fellow men?*"

"Answer. Nowhere do we find a trace of such a difference. See Lev. xix. 33–36.

"God says thou shalt not murder, *steal*, cheat, &c. In every place the action *itself* is prohibited as being an abomination to God *without respect to the persons against whom it is committed.*"

XI. Servants were placed upon a level with
their masters in all civil and religious rights.
Num. xv. 15, 16, 29; ix. 14; Deut. i. 16, 17; Lev.
xxiv. 22. To these may be added that numerous class
of passages which represents God as regarding *alike*
the natural rights of *all* men, and making for all an
*equal* provision. Such as, 2 Chron. xix. 7; Prov.
xxiv. 23, xxviii. 21; Job. xxxiv. 19; 2 Sam. xiv. 14;
Acts x. 35; Eph. vi. 9.

Finally—With such watchful jealousy did the Mosaic Institutes guard the *rights* of servants, as to make
the fact of a servant's escape from his master presumptive evidence that his master had *oppressed* him; they
annulled his master's authority over him, gave him
license to go wherever he pleased, and commanded all
to protect him. Deut. xxiii. 15, 16.

## II. WERE PERSONS MADE SERVANTS AGAINST THEIR WILLS?

We argue that they became servants *of their own
accord*, because,

I. To become a servant was to become a proselyte. He was required to abjure idolatry, to enter
into covenant with God,* be circumcised in token of

* Maimonides, a contemporary with Jarchi, standing with
him at the head of Jewish writers, gives the following testimony on this point:—

"Whether a servant be born in the power of an Israelite,
or whether he be purchased from the heathen, the master is
to bring them both into the covenant.

"But he that is in the *house* is entered on the eighth day,

it, be bound to keep the Sabbath, the Passover, the
Pentecost, and the Feast of Tabernacles, and to
receive instruction in the moral and ceremonial law.
Were the servants *forced* through all these processes?
Was the renunciation of idolatry *compulsory?* Were
they *dragged* into covenant with God? Were they
seized and circumcised by *main strength?* Were they
*compelled* to eat the flesh of the Paschal lamb, while
they abhorred the institution of the Passover, spurned
the laws that enjoined it, detested its author and its
executors, and, instead of rejoicing in the deliverance
which it commemorated, bewailed it as a calamity,

and he that is bought with money, on the day on which his
master receives him, unless the slave be *unwilling.* For if
the master receive a grown slave, and he be *unwilling,* his
master is to bear with him, to seek to win him over by instruction, and by love and kindness, for one year. After .
which, should he *refuse* so long, it is forbidden to keep him
longer than a year. And the master must send him back to
the strangers from whence he came. For the God of Jacob
will not accept any other than the worship of a *willing*
heart."—Maimon., Hilcoth Miloth, Chap. 1, Sec. 8.

The Jewish Doctors assert that the servant from the
Strangers who at the close of his probationary year, refused
to adopt the Jewish religion and was on that account sent
back to his own people, received a *full compensation* for his
services, besides the payment of his expenses. But that
*postponement* of the circumcision of the foreign servant for a
year (*or even at all* after he had entered the family of an Israelite) of which the Mishnic doctors speak, seems to have
been *a mere usage.* We find nothing of it in the regulations
of the Mosaic system. Circumcision was manifestly a rite
strictly *initiatory.* Whether it was a rite merely *national* or
*spiritual,* or *both,* comes not within the scope of this inquiry.

and cursed the day of its consummation ? **Were they**
*driven* from all parts of the land three times in the
year to the annual festivals ? Were they goaded
through a round of ceremonies, to them senseless and
disgusting mummeries; and drilled into the technics of
a creed rank with loathed abominations ? Did God
authorize his people to make proselytes, by the terror
of pains and penalties ? by converting men into *merchandise?* Were *proselyte and chattel* synonymes in
the Divine vocabulary ? Was a man to be sunk to a
*thing* before taken into covenant with God ?

II. THE SURRENDER OF FUGITIVE SERVANTS TO
THEIR MASTERS WAS PROHIBITED. " Thou shalt not
deliver unto his master the servant which is escaped
from his master unto thee. He shall dwell with thee,
even among you, in that place which he shall choose,
in one of thy gates where it liketh him best ; thou shalt
not oppress him." Deut. xxiii. 15, 16.

As though God had said, " To deliver him up would
be to recognize the *right* of the master to hold him ;
his *fleeing* shows his *choice*, proclaims his wrongs and
his title to protection ; you shall not force him back,
and thus recognize the *right* of the master to hold
him in such a condition as impels him to. flee to others
for protection." It may be said that this command
referred only to the servants of *heathen* masters in the
surrounding nations. We answer : the terms of the
command are unlimited. Besides the objection merely
shifts the difficulty. Did God require them to protect
the *free choice* of a *single* servant from the heathen,
and yet *authorize* the same persons to crush the free
choice of *thousands* from the heathen ? Suppose a

5

case. A *foreign* servant escapes to the Israelites ; God
says, " He shall dwell with thee, in that place which
*he shall choose.*" Now, suppose this same servant,
instead of coming into Israel of his own accord, had
been *dragged* in by some kidnapper who bought him
of his master ; would He who forbade such treatment
of the stranger, who *voluntarily* came into the land,
sanction the same treatment of the *same person*, provided in addition to this last outrage, the previous
one had been committed of forcing him into the nation
against his will ?   To commit violence on the free
choice of a foreign servant is, forsooth, a horrible enormity, provided you *begin* the violence *after* he has come
among you !  But if you commit the first act on the
*other side of the line,* by buying him from a third
person, and then tear him from home, drag him into
the land of Israel, and hold him as a slave—ah ! that
alters the case, and you may perpetrate the violence
now with impunity !  Would *greater* favor have been
shown to this new comer than to the old residents—
those who had been servants in Jewish families perhaps for a generation ?  Were the Israelites commanded to exercise towards *him,* uncircumcised and
out of the covenant, a justice and kindness denied to
the multitudes who *were* circumcised, and *within* the
covenant ?  But suppose that the command respected
merely the fugitives from the surrounding nations,
while it left the servants of the Israelites in a condition against their wills.  In that case, they would
adopt retaliatory measures, and become so many
asylums for Jewish fugitives.  As these nations were
on every side of them, and in their midst, such a

proclamation would have been an effectual lure to men held against their will. Besides, the command which protected the servant from the power of his foreign *master*, protected him equally from that of an *Israelite.* It was not merely, "Thou shalt not deliver him unto his *master*," but "he shall dwell with thee, in that place which *he shall choose*, in one of thy gates, where it liketh *him* best." What was this but a proclamation, that all who *chose* to live in the land and obey the laws were left to dispose of their services at such a rate, to such persons, and in such places as they pleased? Besides, grant that this command prohibited the sending back of *foreign* servants only, there was no law requiring the return of servants who had escaped from the *Israelites*. *Property* lost and *cattle* escaped they were required to return, but not escaped *servants*. These verses contain, 1st, a command, "Thou shalt not deliver," &c. ; 2d, a declaration of the fugitive's right of *free choice ;* and 3d, a command guarding this right, namely, "Thou shalt not oppress him," as though God had said, "If ye restrain him from exercising his *own choice*, as to the place and condition of his residence, it is *oppression*, and shall not be tolerated."*

* Perhaps it may be objected that this view of Deut. xxiii. 15, 16, makes nonsense of Ex. xxi. 27, which provides that if a man strikes out his servant's tooth he shall let him go free. Small favor indeed if the servant might set himself free whenever he pleased! Answer—The former passage might remove the servant from the master's *authority*, without annulling the master's legal claims upon the servant, if he had paid him in advance and had not received from him an

III. The servants had peculiar opportunities and facilities for escape. Three times a year, all the males over twelve years were required to attend the national feasts. They were thus absent from their homes not less than three weeks at each time. As these caravans moved, were there scouts lining the way, to intercept deserters?—a guard at each pass of the mountains, sentinels pacing the hilltops, and light-horse scouring the defiles? The Israelites must have had some safe contrivance for taking their "*slaves*" three times in a year to Jerusalem and back. When a body of slaves is moved in our *republic*, they are handcuffed and chained together, to keep them from running away, or from beating their drivers' brains out. Was this the *Mosaic* plan, or an improvement introduced by Samuel, or was it left for the wisdom of Solomon? The usage, doubtless, claims a paternity not less venerable and biblical! Perhaps they were lashed upon camels, and transported in bundles, or caged up and trundled on wheels to and fro, and while at the Holy City, "lodged in jail for safe keeping," the Sanhedrim appointing special religious services for their benefit, and their "drivers" officiating at "ORAL instruction." Meanwhile what became of the sturdy *handmaids* left at home? What hindered them from stalking off in a body? Perhaps the

equivalent, and this equally, whether his master were a Jew or a Gentile. The latter passage, "He shall let him go free *for his tooth's sake*," not only freed the servant from the master's authority, but also from any pecuniary claim which the master may have on account of having paid his wages in advance; and this as a *compensation* for the loss of a tooth.

Israelitish matrons stood sentry in rotation round the kitchens, while the young ladies scoured the country, as mounted rangers, picking up stragglers by day, and patrolled the streets, keeping a sharp lookout at night!

IV. WILFUL NEGLECT OF CEREMONIAL RITES DISSOLVED THE RELATION.

Suppose the servants from the heathen had, upon entering Jewish families, refused circumcision; if *slaves*, how simple the process of emancipation! Or, suppose they had refused to attend the annual feasts, or had eaten leavened bread during the Passover, or compounded the ingredients of the anointing oil, or had touched a dead body, a bone, or a grave, or in any way had contracted ceremonial uncleanness, and refused to be cleansed with the "water of separation," they would have been "cut off from the people;" *excommunicated*. Ex. xii. 19; xxx. 33; Num. xix. 16.

V. SERVANTS OF THE PATRIARCHS NECESSARILY VOLUNTARY. Abraham's servants are an illustration. At one time he had three hundred and eighteen *young men* "born in his house." His servants of both sexes and all ages were probably MANY THOUSANDS. How did Abraham and Sarah contrive to hold so many servants against their wills? Probably the Patriarch and his wife "took turns" in surrounding them! The neighboring tribes, instead of constituting a picket guard to hem in his servants, would have been far more likely to sweep them and him into captivity, as they did Lot and his household. Besides, there was neither a "compact," to send back Abraham's fugi-

5*

tives, nor a truckling police to pounce upon them, nor
gentlemen-kidnappers, suing for his patronage, boast-
ing their blood-hound scent, and promising to hunt
down and deliver up, provided they had a description
of the "flesh marks," and were suitably stimulated by
pieces of silver.* Abraham seems also to have lacked
all the auxiliaries of family government, such as stocks,
hand-cuffs, yokes, gags, and thumb-screws. Yet he
faithfully trained "his household to do justice and
judgment," though so destitute of the needful aids.

Job seems to have had thousands of servants. See
Job. i. 3, 14–19, and xlii. 12. That they stayed with
him of their own accord, the *fact* of their staying
shows. Suppose the whole army had filed off before
him, how could the patriarch have brought them to
a halt? With his wife, seven sons, and three daughters, how soon he would have outflanked the fugitives,

---

* The following is a standing newspaper advertisement of
one of these professional man-catchers, a member of the New
York bar, who plies his trade in the commercial emporium,
sustained by the complacent greetings of "HONORABLE MEN !"

"IMPORTANT TO THE SOUTH.—F. H. Pettis, being located in
the City of New York, in the practice of law, announces to
his friends and the public in general, that he has been engaged as Council and Adviser in General for a party whose
business it is in the northern cities to arrest and secure runaway slaves. He has been thus engaged for several years,
and invites post-paid communications to him, inclosing a fee
of $20 in each case, and a power of attorney minutely
descriptive of the party absconded, and if in the northern
region, he or she will soon be had.

"N. B. New York City is estimated to contain 5,000 runaway slaves.                                    "PETTIS."

and dragged each of them back to his wonted chain and staple.

Besides, we have his own testimony that he had not " withheld from the poor their *desire*." Job. xxxi. 16. Of course he could hardly have forced them to work for him against " *their desire*."

When Isaac sojourned in the country of the Philistines, he "had *great store* of servants." And we have testimony that the Philistines hated and "envied" him. Of course, they would not volunteer to organize patrols to keep his servants from running away, and to drive back all found beyond the limits of his plantation without a "pass?" If Isaac's servants were held against their wills, *who* held them?

The servants of the Jews, during the building of the wall of Jerusalem, may be included under this head. That they remained of their own accord we argue from the fact that circumstances made it impossible to *compel* their service. The Jews were few in number, without resources, defensive fortifications, or munitions of war, and surrounded by a host of foes, scoffing at their feebleness and inviting desertion. Yet the Jews put arms into the hands of their servants, and enrolled them as a night-guard, for the defence of the city. By engaging in this service, when they might all have marched over to the enemy, and been received with shoutings, they testified that their condition was one of *their own choice*. Neh. iv. 23.

VI. No INSTANCES OF ISRAELITISH MASTERS SELLING SERVANTS. Neither Abraham nor Isaac seems ever to have sold one, though they had "great store of servants." Jacob had a large number of servants.

Joseph invited him to come into Egypt, and to bring
with him all that he had—"thou and thy children, and
thy children's children, and thy flocks and thy herds,
and ALL THAT THOU HAST." Gen. xlv. 10. Jacob
took his flocks and herds, but *no servants.* Yet we
are told that he "took his journey with *all that he
had.*" Gen. xlvi. i. Joseph said to Pharaoh, "My
father, and my brethren, and their flocks, and their
herds, and *all that they have,* are come." Gen. xlvii.
1. The servants, doubtless, served under their *own
contracts,* and when Jacob went into Egypt, they *chose*
to stay in their own country.

The government might sell *thieves,* until their services had made good the injury, and paid the legal
fine. Ex. xxii. 3. But *masters* seem to have had no
power to sell their *servants.* To give the master a
*right* to sell his servants would annihilate the servant's
right of choice in his own disposal. But, says the
objector, "to give the master a right to *buy* a servant,
equally annihilates the servant's *right of choice.*"
Answer. It is one thing to have a right to buy a
man, and quite another thing to have a right to buy
him of *another* man.

Young females were bought of their *fathers.* But
their purchase as *servants* was their betrothal as
WIVES. Ex. xxi. 7, 8. "If a man sell his daughter
to be a maid-servant, she shall not go out as the men-
servants do. If she please not her master WHO HATH
BETROTHED HER TO HIMSELF, he shall let her be redeemed."*

* The comment of Maimonides on this passage is as follows : "A Hebrew bondmaid might not be sold but to one who

VII. VOLUNTARY SERVANTS FROM THE STRANGERS.

We infer that *all* the servants from the strangers were voluntary, since we have direct testimony that some of them were, "Thou shalt not oppress an hired servant that is poor and needy, whether he be of thy brethren, OR OF THY STRANGERS that are in thy land within thy gates." Deut. xxiv. 14. We learn from this that some of the servants from the strangers, were procured by the offer of *wages* to their *free choice*. Did the Israelites, when they went among the heathen to procure servants, take money in one hand and ropes in the other? Did they *ask* one man, and *drag* along another, in spite of his struggle? Knock for admission at one door, and break down the next? Did they go through one village with friendly salutations, offering wages as an inducement to engage in their service—while they prowled through the next, with a kidnapping posse, tearing from their homes all they could get within their clutches?

VIII. HEBREW SERVANTS VOLUNTARY. We infer that the Hebrew servant was voluntary in COMMENCING his services, because he was SO IN CONTINUING it. If, at the year of release, it was the servant's *choice* to remain with his master, the law required his ear to be bored by the judges, and his master was *compelled* to keep him.

laid himself under obligations to espouse her to himself or to his son, when she was fit to be betrothed."—*Maimonides— Hilcoth—Obedim*, Ch. IV. Sec. XI. Jarchi, on the same passage, says, "He is bound to espouse her to be his wife, for the *money of her purchase* is the money of her *espousal*."

IX. THE MANNER OF PROCURING SERVANTS WAS AN
APPEAL TO CHOICE. The Israelites might neither seize
them by *force,* nor frighten them by *threats,* nor
wheedle them by false pretences ; but they were to BUY
them—that is, they were to recognize the *right* of the
individuals to *dispose* of their own services, and their
right to *refuse all offers.* Suppose all had *refused*
to become servants, what provision did the Mosaic
law make for such an emergency ? NONE.

X. INCIDENTAL CORROBORATIVES. Various incidental expressions corroborate the idea that servants
became such by their own contract. Job xli. 4, is an
illustration, " Will he (Leviathan) make a COVENANT
with thee ? wilt thou take him for a SERVANT forever ?" So Isa. xiv. 1, 2. " The strangers shall be
joined with them (the Israelites), and *they shall*
CLEAVE to the house of Jacob, and the house of Israel
shall possess them in the land of the Lord for servants
and handmaids."

The transaction which made the Egyptians the
SERVANTS OF PHARAOH was voluntary throughout.
See Gen. xlvii. 18–26. " There is not aught left but
our *bodies* and our lands ; *buy* us ;" then " We will be
Pharaoh's servants."

Our Lord's declaration in Luke xvi. 13, loses its
pertinence on the supposition that servants did not
become such by *their own choice.* " No servant can
serve two masters : for either he will hate the one and
love the other, or else he will hold to the one and
despise the other." Our Lord was a *Jew.* Wherever he went Jews were around him : whenever he
spake, they were his auditors. His preaching and

teaching were full of illustrations drawn from their
own institutions. In the verse quoted, he illustrates
the impossibility of their making choice of God as
their portion, and becoming his servants while they
choose the world, and are *its* servants. To make this
clear, he refers to their own institution of *domestic
service.* He reminds them of the impossibility of any
person being the servant of two masters, as he will
*choose* the service of the one, and *spurn* that of the
other. " He shall *hold to* the one and *despise* (reject)
the other." As though our Lord had said, " No one
can become the servant of another, when his will
revolts from that service, and the conditions of it tend
to make him hate the man." Since the fact that the
servant *spurns* one of two masters, makes it impossible for him to serve *that one,* if he spurned *both,* he
could not serve *either.* So, also, if the fact that an
individual did not "hold to" or choose the service of
another, proves that he could not become his servant,
then the question, whether he should become the
servant of another was suspended on *his own will.*
The phraseology of the passage shows that the *choice*
of the servant decided the question. " He will HOLD
TO the one"—hence there is no difficulty in the way
of his serving *him;* but "no servant can serve" a
master whom he does not "*hold to,*" or *cleave* to.
This is the sole ground of the impossibility asserted.

The last clause of the verse is an application of the
principle, "Ye cannot serve God and mammon." In
what does the impossibility of serving both God and
the world consist ? Solely in the fact, that the will
which chooses the one refuses the other, and the affec-

tions which "hold to" the one, reject the other.
Thus the question, which of the two is to be served, is
suspended upon the choice of the individual.

XI. RICH STRANGERS DID NOT BECOME SERVANTS.
Indeed, they bought and held Jewish servants.  Lev.
xxv. 47.   Since *rich* strangers did not become servants, we infer that those who *did*, became such not
because they were *strangers*, but because they were
*poor*—not because being heathens, they were *compelled* to become servants, but because on account
of their *poverty*, they *chose* to thus better their condition.

XII. INSTANCES OF VOLUNTARY SERVANTS.   Mention is often made of persons becoming servants who
were manifestly VOLUNTARY.   As the Prophet Elisha.
1 Kings xix. 21 ; 2 Kings iii. 11.   Elijah was his
*master*.   2 Kings ii. 5.   The word translated master,
is the same that is so rendered in almost every instance
where masters are spoken of.   Moses was the servant
of Jethro.   Ex. iii. 1 ; iv. 10.   Joshua was the
servant of Moses.   Ex. xxxiii. 11 ; Num. xi. 28.
Jacob was the servant of Laban.   Gen. xxix. 18–27.
See also the case of the Gibeonites who *voluntarily*
became servants, and performed service for the "house
of God" throughout the subsequent Jewish history,
were incorporated with the Israelites, registered in
their genealogies, and of their own accord remained
with them, and "*clave*" to them.   Neh. x. 28, 29 ;
xi. 3 ; Ez. vii. 7.

Finally, in all the regulations respecting servants
no expression is used indicating that servants were
made, and held such by force.   Add to this the

absence of all the machinery, appurtenances and incidents of *compulsion*.

Voluntary service is in keeping with· regulations which abounded in the Mosaic system, and is sustained by a multitude of analogies. Compulsory service could have harmonized with nothing, and would have been the solitary disturbing force, marring its design, counteracting its tendencies, and confusing and falsifying its types. The directions regulating the performance of service for the *public* lay great stress on the *willingness* of those employed. For the spirit of the Mosaic system in this respect, see 1 Chron. xxviii. 21; Ex. xxxv. 5, 21, 22, 29; 1 Chron. xxix. 5, 6, 9, 14, 17; Ex. xxv. 2; Judges v. 2; Lev. xxii. 29; 2 Chron. xxxv. 8; Ezra i. 6; Ex. xxxv. ; Neh. xi. 2.*

The voluntariness of servants is a natural inference from the fact that the Hebrew word *ebĕdh*, uniformly rendered *servant,* is applied to many classes of persons, *all of whom* were voluntary and most of them eminently so. It is applied to persons rendering acts of *worship* about seventy times, whereas it is applied to *servants* not more than half that number of times.

The illustrations drawn from the condition of *servants,* and the ideas which the term is employed to convey when applied figuratively, would, in most

* We should naturally infer that the directions which regulated service to individuals would proceed upon the same principle, in this respect, with those regulating service to the *public*. Otherwise, the Mosaic system would be divided against itself; its principles counteracting and nullifying each other.

6

instances, lose their force, and often become absurdi-
ties if the will of the servant *resisted* his service, and
he performed it by *compulsion*.   We give a single
example:   "*To whom* YE YIELD YOURSELVES *servants
to obey, his servants ye are to whom ye obey.*"   Rom.
vi. 16.   It would be difficult to assert the voluntariness of servants more strongly in a direct proposition
than it is here done by implication.

### III.   WERE SERVANTS FORCED TO WORK WITHOUT PAY?

As the servants became and continued such of *their
own accord,* it would be no small marvel if they *chose*
to work without pay.   Their becoming servants presupposes *compensation* as a motive.   That they *were
paid* for their labor, we argue—

I. BECAUSE GOD REBUKED THE USING OF SERVICE
WITHOUT WAGES.   "Wo unto him that buildeth his
house by unrighteousness, and his chambers by wrong;
THAT USETH HIS NEIGHBOR'S SERVICE WITHOUT WAGES,
AND GIVETH HIM NOT FOR HIS WORK."   Jer. xxii. 13.
The Hebrew word *reā,* translated *neighbor,* means
any one with whom we have to do—all descriptions
of persons, even enemies while fighting us.   See Deut.
xxii. 26; Prov. xxv. 8; Ex. xx. 16; Ex. xxi. 14,
&c.   The doctrine inculcated in this passage is, that
every man's labor, being his own property, he is
entitled to the profit of it, and that for another to
"use" it, without paying him the value of it, is "unrighteousness."   The last clause of the verse, "and
giveth him not for his work," reaffirms the same prin-

ciple, that every man is to be *paid* for "his work."
In the context, the prophet contrasts the unrighteousness of those who used the labor of others without
pay, with the justice practised by their patriarchal
ancestor. "Did not thy father eat and drink, and
*do judgment and justice;* and then it was well with
him? He *judged the cause of the poor and needy.*
But thine eyes and thine heart are not but for thy
*covetousness,* and for *oppression,* and for violence to
do it." Jer. xxii. 15, 16, 17.*

II. God testifies that in our duty to our
fellow-men, all the law and the prophets hang
upon this command, "Thou shalt love thy neighbor as thyself." This is *verbatim* one of the laws
of the Mosaic system. Lev. xix. 18. Moses applies
this law to the treatment of strangers: "The stranger
that dwelleth with you shall be unto you as one born
among you, and thou shalt love him as thyself."
If it be loving others *as* ourselves to make them work
for us without pay; to rob them of food, and clothing
also, would be a still stronger illustration of the law
of love! And if it be doing unto others as we would

* Paul says: "Masters, give unto your servants that
which is just and equal." Col. iv. 1. Thus not only asserting the *right* of the servant and the duty of the master, but
condemning all those relations between them which were
not founded upon justice and equality of rights. James
enforces the same principle. "Behold, the hire of the
laborers, who have reaped down your fields, which is of you
kept back *by fraud,* crieth." James v. 4. As though he
had said, "wages are the *right* of laborers; this you refuse to
render, and thus *defraud* them." See also Mal. iii. 5.

have them do to us to make them work for *our own*
good alone, Paul should be called to order for his
hard sayings against human nature, especially for that
libel in Eph. v. 22 : " No man ever yet hated his own
flesh, but nourisheth it and cherisheth it."

III. SERVANTS WERE OFTEN WEALTHY.   As persons
became servants FROM POVERTY, we argue that they
were compensated, since they frequently owned property, and sometimes a large amount.   Ziba, the
servant of Mephibosheth, gave David "two hundred
loaves of bread, and a hundred bunches of raisins, and
a hundred of summer fruits, and a bottle of wine."
2 Sam. xvi. 1.   He had twenty servants.   In Lev.
xxv. 47–49, where a servant, reduced to poverty, sold
himself, it is declared that he may be *redeemed*, either
by his kindred or by HIMSELF.   Having been forced
to sell himself from poverty, he must have acquired
considerable property *after* he became a servant.   If
it had not been common for servants to acquire property, the servant of Elisha would hardly have ven-
tured to take a large sum of money (nearly $3000)
from Naaman : 2 Kings v. 22, 23.   As it was procured by deceit, he wished to conceal the means used
in getting it ; but if servants could " own nothing, nor
acquire anything," to embark in such an enterprise
would have been consummate stupidity.   The fact of
having in his possession two talents of silver would,
of itself, convict him of theft.*   But since it was com-

---

* Whoever heard of slaves stealing a large amount of
money ?   When they steal, they are careful to do it on such
a *small* scale, or in the taking of *such things* as will make

mon for servants to own property, he might have, invest, or use it without attracting especial attention, and that alone would be a motive to the act. His master not only does not take it from him, but seems to expect that he would invest it in real estate and cattle, and would procure servants with it. 2 Kings v. 26. We find the servant of Saul having money, and with it relieving his master in an emergency. 1 Sam. ix. 8. Arza, the servant of Elah, was the *owner of a house.* That it was somewhat magnificent would be a natural inference from its being a resort of the king. 1 Kings xvi. 9. When Jacob became the servant of Laban, it was evidently from poverty; yet Laban said to him, Tell me "what shall thy *wages* be?" After Jacob had been his servant for ten years, he proposed to set up for himself; but Laban said,

detection difficult. No doubt they steal. Why shouldn't they follow in the footsteps of their masters and mistresses? Dull scholars indeed! if, after so many lessons from *proficients* in the art, they should not occasionally try their hand in a small way, the *only permanent and general* business carried on around them! Ignoble truly! never to imitate the "Honorables" and "Excellencies," Doctors of Divinity, and *Right* and *Very Reverends!* Hear President Jefferson's testimony. In his *Notes on Virginia,* pp. 207–8, speaking of slaves, he says, "That disposition to theft with which they have been branded must be ascribed to their *situation,* and not to any special depravity of the moral sense. It is a problem which I give the master to solve, whether the religious precepts against the violation of property were not framed for HIM as well as for his slave, and whether the slave may not as justifiably take a *little* from one who has taken ALL from him, as he may *slay* one who would slay him?"

6*

"Appoint me thy wages, and I will give it." During
the twenty years that Jacob was a servant, he always
worked for wages, and at his own price. Gen. xxix.
15, 18 ; xxx. 28–33. The case of the Gibeonites,
who, after becoming servants, still occupied their
cities, and remained in many respects a distinct people for centuries ;* and that of the 150,000 Canaanites, the *servants* of Solomon, who worked out their
"tribute of bond-service" in levies, periodically relieving each other, are additional illustrations of independence in the acquisition and ownership of property.

Again. The Israelites often *hired* servants from
the strangers. Deut. xxiv. 17.

Since then they give wages to a part of their Canaanitish servants, thus recognizing their *right* to a reward
for their labor, we infer that they did not rob the rest
of their earnings.

If God gave them a license to make the strangers
work for them without pay, what fools to pay wages
when they could make the strangers work for nothing !
Besides, by refusing to avail themselves of this
"Divine license," they despised the blessing, and cast
contempt on the giver ! But perhaps the Israelites
seized all the Canaanites they could lay their hands
on, and forced them to work without pay, but not
being able to catch enough, were obliged to offer
wages in order to eke out the supply !

---

* The Nethinims, which name was afterwards given to the
Gibeonites on account of their being *set apart* for the service
of the tabernacle, had their own houses and cities, and
"dwelt every one in his own possession." Neh. xi. 3, 21 ;
Ezra ii. 70 ; 1 Chron. ix. 2.

The parable in Mat. xviii. 23–34 derives its significance from the fact, that servants could *own*, *owe*, and *earn* property, and it would be made a medley of contradictions on any other supposition.—1. Their lord at a set time proceeded to "take account" and "reckon" with his servants; the phraseology showing that the relations between the parties were those of debt and credit. 2. One of his servants was found to *owe* him ten thousand talents. From the fact that the servant *owed* this to his master, we infer that he must have been the *owner* of that amount, or of its substantial equivalent; that having sustained the responsibilities of legal *proprietorship*, he was under the liabilities resulting therefrom. 3. Not having, then, wherewith to pay, he says to his master, "Have patience with me, *and I will pay thee all.*" If the servant were his master's *property*, his time and earnings were the master's; hence the promise to earn and pay that amount was virtually saying, "I will take money out of your pocket to pay my debt to you." The promise to pay the debt, on condition that the payment should be postponed, proceeds upon the fact that his time was his own, that he was earning property or in circumstances to earn it, that he was the *proprietor* of his earnings, and that his master had *full knowledge* of that fact. The supposition that the master was the *owner* of the servant would annihilate all legal claim upon him; and that the servant was the *property* of his master would absolve him from all obligations of debt, or rather *forestall* such obligations—for the relations of owner and creditor would annihilate each other, as would those of *pro-*

*perty* and *debtor*. The fact that the same servant was the creditor of one of his fellow-servants, who owed him a considerable sum, and that at last he was imprisoned until he should pay all that was due to his master, are additional corroborations.

IV. HEIRSHIP.—Servants frequently inherited their master's property; especially if he had no sons, or if they had dishonored the family. Eliezer, the servant of Abraham—Gen. xv. 23; Ziba, the servant of Mephibosheth; Jarha, the servant of Sheshan, who married his daughter, and thus became his heir, he having no sons; and the *husbandmen* who said of their master's son, "This is the HEIR; let us kill him, and the INHERITANCE WILL BE OURS," are illustrations; also Prov. xxx. 23, "An *handmaid* (or *maid servant*) that is *heir* to her mistress;" also Prov. xvii. 2—"A wise servant shall have rule over a son that causeth shame, and SHALL HAVE PART OF THE INHERITANCE AMONG THE BRETHREN." This passage gives servants precedence as heirs, even over the wives and daughters of their masters. Did masters hold by force, and plunder of earnings, a class of persons from which, in frequent contingencies, they selected both heirs for their property, and husbands for their daughters?

V. ALL WERE REQUIRED TO PRESENT OFFERINGS AND SACRIFICES. Deut. xvi. 16, 17; 2 Chron. xv. 9–11; Num. ix. 13, 14. Beside this, "every man," from twenty years old and above, was required to pay a tax of half a shekel; this is called "offering unto the Lord to make an atonement for their souls." Ex. xxx. 12 –16. See also Ex. xxxiv. 20. Servants must have had permanently the means of *acquiring* property to meet these expenditures.

VI. SERVANTS WHO WENT OUT AT THE SEVENTH YEAR WERE "FURNISHED LIBERALLY." Deut. xv. 10 –14. "Thou shalt furnish him liberally out of thy flock, and out of thy floor, and out of thy wine press :"* If it be said that the servants from the strangers did not receive a like bountiful supply, we answer, neither did the most honorable class of *Israelitish* servants, the free-holders ; and for the same reason, *they did not go out in the seventh year*, but continued until the jubilee.

VII. SERVANTS WERE BOUGHT. In other words, they received compensation in advance.† Having

---

* The comment of Maimonides on this passage is as follows: "'Thou shalt furnish him liberally,' &c. That is to say, '*Loading, ye shall load him*,' likewise every one of his family, with as much as he can take with him—abundant benefits. And if it be avariciously asked, ' How much must I give him ?' I say unto *you, not less than thirty shekels*— which is the valuation of a servant, as declared in Ex. xxi. 32."—*Maimonides, Hilcoth Obedim*, chap. ii. sec. 3.

† But, says the objector, if servants received their pay in advance, and if the Israelites were forbidden to surrender the fugitive to his master, it would operate practically as a motive to servants to make contracts, get their pay in advance, and then run away. We answer, the prohibition, Deut. xxiii. 15, 16, " Thou shalt not deliver unto his master," &c., sets the servant free from his *authority*, and, of course, from all those liabilities to injury, to which, *as his servant*, he was subjected, but not from the obligation of legal contracts. If the servant had received pay in advance, and had not rendered an equivalent for this " value received," he was not absolved from his obligation to do so, but from all obligation

shown that servants *sold themselves*, except in cases
where parents hired out the time of their children till
they became of age,* a mere reference to the fact
is all that is required for the purposes of this argument.

VIII. THE RIGHT OF SERVANTS TO COMPENSATION IS
RECOGNIZED IN Ex. xxi. 27. "And if he smite out
his man-servant's or his maid-servant's tooth, he shall
let him go free for his tooth's sake." This regulation
is founded upon the *right* of the servant to the *use* of
all his powers, and consequently, his just claim for
remuneration upon him, who should, however *uninten-
tionally*, deprive him of the least of them. If the
servant had a right to his *tooth* and the *use* of it, he
had a right to the rest of his body and the use of it.
If he had a right to the *fraction* to hold, use, and
have pay for, he had a right to the *sum total.*

IX. WE FIND MASTERS AT ONE TIME HAVING A
LARGE NUMBER OF SERVANTS, AND AFTERWARDS NONE,
WITH NO INTIMATION IN ANY CASE THAT THEY WERE
SOLD. The wages of servants would enable them to
set up in business for themselves. Jacob, after being
Laban's servant for twenty-one years, became an
independent herdsman, and had many servants. Gen.
xxx. 43; xxxii. 16. But all these had left him before
he went into Egypt. Gen. xlv. 10, 11; xlvi. 1–7, 32.
The case of Ziba, the servant who had twenty servants,
has been already mentioned.

to pay his master in *that particular way;* that is, *by working
for him as his servant.*

\* Among the Israelites, girls became of age at twelve, and
boys at thirteen years.

X. GOD'S TESTIMONY TO THE CHARACTER OF ABRA-
HAM. Gen. xviii. 19. "For I know him that he
will command his children, and his household after
him, and they shall keep THE WAY OF THE LORD TO DO
JUSTICE AND JUDGMENT." What was "the way of the
Lord" respecting wages where service was rendered?
"Wo unto him that useth his neighbor's service WITH-
OUT WAGES!" Jer. xxii. 13. "Masters, give unto
your servants that which is JUST AND EQUAL." Col.
iv. 1. "Render unto all their DUES." Rom. xiii. 7.
"The laborer is WORTHY OF HIS HIRE." Luke x. 7.
How did Abraham teach his servants to "*do justice*"
to others? By doing injustice to *them*? Did he
exhort them to "render to all their dues" by keeping
back *their own*? Did he teach them that "the
laborer was worthy of his hire" by robbing them of
*theirs*? Did he beget in them a reverence for honesty
by pilfering all their time and labor? Did he teach
them "not to defraud" others "in any matter" by
denying *them* "what was just and equal?" If each
of Abraham's pupils did not under such a catechism
become a very *Aristides* in justice, then illustrious
examples, patriarchal dignity, and *practical* lessons,
can make but slow headway against human perverse-
ness!

XI. SPECIFIC PRECEPTS OF THE MOSAIC LAW
ENFORCING GENERAL PRINCIPLES. Out of many we
select the following: (1.) "Thou shalt not muzzle the
ox when he treadeth out the corn." Deut. xxv. 4.
Here is a general principle applied to a familiar case.
The ox representing all workers. Isa. xxx. 24. A
*particular* kind of service, *all* kinds; and a law

requiring an abundant provision for the wants of an
animal ministering to a man in a *certain* way—a
general principle of treatment covering all times,
modes, and instrumentalities of service. The object
of the law was not mainly to enjoin tenderness towards
brutes, but to inculcate the duty of rewarding those
who serve us ; and if such care be enjoined, by God,
for the ample sustenance and enjoyment of *a brute,*
what would be a meet return for the services of *man?*
MAN with his varied wants, exalted nature, and immortal destiny ! Paul says that this principle under-
lies the statute. 1 Cor. ix. 9, 10 : "For it is written
in the law of Moses, Thou shalt not muzzle the mouth
of the ox that treadeth out the corn. Doth God take
care for oxen ? Or saith he it altogether for OUR
sakes ? that he that ploweth should plow in HOPE, and
that he that thresheth in hope should be PARTAKER OF
HIS HOPE." In the context, Paul enumerates the
four grand divisions of labor among the Jews in illustration of the principle that the laborer is entitled to
a *reward.* The priests, Levites, and all engaged in
sacred things—the military, those who tended flocks
and herds, and those who cultivated the soil. As the
latter employment engaged the great body of the
Israelites, he amplifies his illustration under that head,
and enumerates the five great departments of agricultural labor among the Jews—vine-dressing, plowing,
sowing, reaping, and threshing, as the representatives
of universal labor. In his epistle to Timothy—1 Tim.
v. 18—Paul quotes again this precept of the Mosaic
law, and connects with it the declaration of our Lord.
Luke x. 7 : "The laborer is worthy of his hire"—as

both inculcating the *same* doctrine, that he who labors, whatever the employment, is entitled to a reward. He thus declares the principle of right respecting service, and the rule of duty towards those who serve, to be the same under both dispensations. (2.) "If thy brother be waxen poor, and fallen in decay with thee, then thou shalt relieve him; YEA, THOUGH HE BE A STRANGER or a SOJOURNER, that he may live with thee. Take thou no usury of him, or increase, but fear thy God. Thou shalt not give him thy money upon usury, nor lend him thy victuals for increase." Lev. xxv. 35–37. By what pro-slavery legerdemain can this regulation be made to harmonize with the doctrine of WORK WITHOUT PAY? Did God declare the poor stranger entitled to RELIEF, and yet authorize others to "use his service without wages."

### IV.—WERE MASTERS THE PROPRIETORS OF SERVANTS AS THEIR LEGAL PROPERTY?

This topic has been somewhat anticipated, but additional considerations remain to be noticed.

I. SERVANTS WERE NOT SUBJECTED TO THE USES NOR LIABLE TO THE CONTINGENCIES OF PROPERTY. 1. *They were never taken in payment for their masters' debts.* Children were sometimes taken (without legal authority) for the debts of a father. 2 Kings iv. 1; Job xxiv. 9; Isa. l. 1; Matt. xviii. 25. Creditors took from debtors property of all kinds, to satisfy their demands. In Job xxiv. 3, cattle are taken; Prov. xxii. 27, household furniture; Lev. xxv. 25–28, the productions of the soil; Lev. xxv. 27–30, houses; Ex. xxii.

7

26, 27; Deut. xxiv. 10–13; Matt. v. 40, clothing; but
*servants* were taken in *no instance.* 2. *Servants were
never given as pledges.* *Property* of all kinds was
pledged for value received ; household furniture, clothing, cattle, money, signets, personal ornaments, &c.
3. *Servants were not put into the hands of others, or
consigned to their keeping.* The precept giving directions how to proceed in a case where property that has
life is delivered to another "to keep," and "it die or
be hurt or driven away," enumerates oxen, asses,
sheep or "any *beast*," but not *servants.* Ex. xxii. 10.
4. *All lost property was to be restored.* Oxen, asses,
sheep, raiment, and "all lost things," are specified—
servants *not.* Deut. xxii. 1–3. Besides, the Israelites
were forbidden to return the runaway servant. Deut.
xxiii 15. 5. *Servants were not sold.* When by fla-
grant misconduct they had forfeited their membership
in an Israelitish family, they were not sold, but *expelled.* Luke xvi. 2–4 ; 2 Kings v. 20, 27 ; Gen. xxi.
14. 6. *The Israelites never received servants as
tribute.* At different times, all the nations around
them were their tributaries. They received property
of all kinds in payment of tribute. Gold, silver, brass,
iron, precious stones, and vessels, armor, spices, raiment, harness, horses, mules, sheep, goats, &c., are in
various places enumerated, but *servants* never. 7. *The
Israelites never gave away their servants.* They made
costly presents, of great variety. Lands, houses, all
kinds of domestic animals, beds, merchandise, family
utensils, precious metals, grain, honey, butter, cheese,
fruits, oil, wine, raiment, armor, &c., are among their
recorded *gifts.* Giving presents to superiors and per-

sons of rank was a standing usage.   1 Sam. x. 27 ; xvi.
20 ; 2 Chron. xvii. 5.    Abraham to Abimelech, Gen.
xxi. 27 ; Jacob to the viceroy of Egypt, Gen. xliii. 11 ;
Joseph to his brethren and father, Gen. xlv. 22, 23 ;
Benhadad to Elisha, 2 Kings viii. 8, 9 ; Ahaz to Tig-
lath Pilezer, 2 Kings vi. 8 ; Solomon to the Queen of
Sheba, 1 Kings x. 13 ; Jeroboam to Ahijah, 1 Kings
xiv. 3 ; Asa to Benhadad, 1 Kings xv. 18, 19 ; Abigail, the wife of Nabal, to David, 1 Sam. xxv. 18 ;
David to the elders of Judah, 1 Sam. xxx. 26 ; Je-
hoshaphat to his sons, 2 Chron. xxi. 3 ; The Israelites
to David, 1 Chron. xii. 39, 40 ; Shobi, Machir, and
Barzillai, to David, 2 Sam. xvii. 28, 29.    But no servants were given as presents, though it was a prevail-
ing fashion in the surrounding nations.    Gen. xii. 16,
xx. 14.    In the last passage we are told that Abimelech, king of the Philistines, "took sheep, and oxen,
and men-servants, and women-servants, and gave them
unto Abraham."    Not long after this Abraham made
Abimelech a present, but gave him *no servants.*
"And Abraham took sheep and oxen, and gave them
unto Abimelech."    Gen. xxi. 27.    It may be objected,
that Laban "GAVE" handmaids to his daughters,
Jacob's wives.    Suffice it to say that the handmaids
of wives were regarded as wives, though of inferior
dignity and authority.    That Jacob so regarded his
handmaids is proved by his curse upon Reuben.    Gen.
xlix. 4, and 1 Chron. v. 1 ; also by the equality of
their children with those of Rachel and Leah.    But
had it been otherwise—had Laban given them *as articles of property*—then, indeed, the example of this
"good old slaveholder and patriarch," Saint Laban,

would have been a forecloser to all argument! Ah! we remember his jealousy for *religion*—his holy indig- nation when he found that his "GODS" were stolen! How he mustered his clan, and plunged over the desert in hot pursuit seven days by forced marches; how he ransacked a whole caravan, sifting the contents of every tent, little heeding such small matters as domes- tic privacy; for, lo! the zeal of his "IMAGES" had eaten him up! No wonder that slavery, in its Bible- navigation, drifting dismantled before the free gusts, should scud under the lee of such a pious worthy, to haul up and refit; invoking his protection and the benediction of his "GODS!" Again, it may be ob- jected, that servants were enumerated in inventories of property. If that proves *servants* property, it proves *wives* property. "Thou shalt not covet thy neighbor's house, thou shalt not covet thy neighbor's WIFE, nor his man-servant, nor his maid-servant, nor his ox, nor his ass, nor anything that is thy neigh- bor's." Ex. xx. 17. In inventories of mere property, if servants are included, it is in such a way as to show that they are not regarded as property. Eccl. ii. 7, 8. But when the design is to show, not merely the wealth, but the sway of any one, servants are spoken of, as well as property. If *riches* alone are spoken of, no mention is made of servants; if sway, servants, and property. Gen. xiii. 2, 5. "And Abraham was very rich in cattle, in silver, and in gold." Yet we are told, in the verse preceding, that he came up out of Egypt "with *all* that he had." "And Lot also had flocks, and herds, and tents." In the seventh verse servants are mentioned: "And there was a strife between the

HERDMEN of Abraham's cattle and the HERDMEN of
Lot's cattle." It is said of Isaac, "And the man
waxed *great*, and went forward, and grew until he became *very great.* For he had possession of flocks,
and possession of herds, and *great store of servants.*"
In immediate connection with this, we find Abimelech,
the king of the Philistines, saying to him, "Thou art
much *mightier* than we." Shortly after this avowal,
Isaac is waited upon by Abimelech, Phicol, the chief
captain of his army, and Ahuzzath, who say, "Let there
now be an oath betwixt us and thee, that thou wilt *do
us no hurt.*" Gen. xxvi. 13, 14, 16, 26, 28, 29. A
plain concession of the *power* which Isaac had in his
"great store of *servants;*" that is, of adherents to
him as a just and benevolent prince. When Hamor
and Shechem speak to the Hivites of the *riches* of
Abraham and his sons, they say, "Shall not their
*cattle,* and their *substance,* and *every beast of theirs*
be ours?" Gen. xxxiv. 23. See also Josh. xxii. 8;
Gen. xxxiv. 23; Job. xlii. 12; 2 Chron. xxi. 3;
xxxii. 27–29; Job. i. 3–5; Deut. viii. 12–17; Gen.
xxiv. 35; xxvi. 13; xxx. 43. Jacob's wives say
to him, "All the *riches* which God has taken from our
father that is ours and our children's." Then follows
an inventory of property—"All his cattle," "all his
goods," "the cattle of his getting." His numerous
servants are not included with his property. Comp.
Gen. xxx. 43, with Gen. xxxi. 16–18. When Jacob
sent messengers to Esau, wishing to impress him with
an idea of his state and sway, he bade them tell him
not only of his RICHES, but of his GREATNESS; that
he had "oxen, and asses, and flocks, and men-servants,

and maid-servants." Gen. xxxii. 4, 5. Yet in the
present which he sent, there were no servants; though
he selected the *most valuable* kinds of property. Gen.
xxxii. 14, 15; see also Gen. xxxvi. 6, 7; xxxiv. 23.
As flocks and herds were the staples of wealth, a large
number of servants presupposed large possessions of
cattle, which would require many herdsmen. When
Jacob and his sons went into Egypt, it is repeatedly
asserted that they took *all that they had.* " Their
cattle and their goods which they had gotten in the
land of Canaan," "their flocks and their herds" are
mentioned, but no *servants.* And as we have, besides,
a full catalogue of the *household,* we know that he
took with him no servants. That Jacob *had* many servants before his migration into Egypt, we learn from
Gen. xxx. 43; xxxii. 5, 16, 19. That he was not the
*proprietor* of these servants is a probable inference from
the fact that he did not take them with him, since we
are told that he did take all his *property.* Gen. xlv.
10; xlvi. 1, 32; xlvii. 1. When servants are spoken
of in connection with *property,* the terms used to express the latter do not include the former. The Hebrew word *miknĕ* is an illustration. It is derived from
*kānā,* to procure, to buy, and its meaning is, a *possession, wealth, riches.* It occurs more than forty times
in the Old Testament, and is applied always to *mere
property,* generally to domestic animals, but never to
servants. In some instances, servants are mentioned
in distinction from the *miknĕ.* "And Abraham took
Sarah, his wife, and Lot, his brother's son, and all
their SUBSTANCE that they had gathered; and the souls
they had gotten in Haran, and they went forth to go

into the land of Canaan." Gen. xii. 5. Many will
have it that these *souls* were a part of Abraham's
*substance* (notwithstanding the pains here taken to
separate them from it)—that they were slaves taken
with him as a part of his family effects. Who but
slaveholders, either actually or in heart, would torture
into the principle and practice of slavery, such a harm-
less phrase as "*the souls that they had gotten?*" Until
the African slave trade breathed its haze into the eyes
of the Church, commentators saw no slavery in "the
souls that they had gotten." In the Targum of Onkelos*
it is rendered, "The souls whom they had brought to
obey the law in Haran." In the Targum of Jonathan,
"The souls whom they had made proselytes in Haran."
In the Targum of Jerusalem, "The souls proselyted
in Haran." Jarchi, the prince of Jewish commentators, "The souls whom they had brought under the
Divine wings." Jerome, one of the most learned of
the Christian fathers, "The persons whom they had
proselyted." The Persian version, the Vulgate, the
Syriac, the Arabic, and the Samaritan, all render it,

---

* The Targums are Chaldee paraphrases of parts of the
Old Testament. The Targum of Onkelos is, for the most part,
a very accurate and faithful translation of the original, and
was probably made at about the commencement of the Christian era. The Targum of Jonathan Ben Uzziel bears about
the same date. The Targum of Jerusalem was probably about
five hundred years later. The Israelites, during their captivity in Babylon, lost, as a body, their own language. These
translations into the Chaldee, the language which they acquired in Babylon, were thus called for by the necessity of
the case.

"All the wealth which they had gathered, and the souls which they had made in Haran." Menochius, a commentator who wrote before our present translation of the Bible, renders it, " *Quas de idolatraria converterant.*" "Those whom they had converted from idolatry." Paulus Fagius,* " *Quas instituerant in religione.*" "Those whom they had established in religion." Luke Francke, a German commentator who lived two centuries ago, " *Quas legi subjicerant.*" "Those whom they had brought to obey the law." The same distinction is made between *persons* and property, in the enumeration of Esau's household and the inventory of his effects. "And Esau took his wives, and his sons, and his daughters, and all the *persons* of his house, and his cattle, and all his beasts, and all his *substance* which he had got in the land of Canaan, and went into the country from the face of his brother Jacob. For their *riches* were more than that they might dwell together; and the land could not bear them because of their *cattle.*" Gen. xxxvi. 6, 7.

II. The condition and social estimation of servants make the doctrine that they were commodities, an absurdity. As the head of a Jewish family possessed the same power over his wife, children, and grandchildren (if in his family) as over

---

* This eminent Hebrew scholar was invited to England to superintend the translation of the Bible into English, under the patronage of Henry the Eighth. He had hardly commenced the work when he died—nearly a century before the date of our present translation.

his servants, if the latter were articles of property, the former were equally such. If there were nothing else in the Mosaic institutes establishing the social equality of the servants with their masters' wives and children, those precepts which required that they should be guests at all the public feasts, and equal participants in the family and social rejoicings, would be quite sufficient to settle the question. Deut. xii. 12, 18; xvi. 10, 11, 13, 14; Ex. xii. 43, 44. Paul's testimony in Gal. iv. 1, shows the condition of servants : "Now I say unto you, that the heir, so long as he is a child, DIFFERETH NOTHING FROM A SERVANT, though he be lord of all." That the interests of Abraham's servants were identified with those of their master's family, and that the utmost confidence was reposed in them, is shown in their being armed.   Gen. xiv. 14, 15.   When Abraham's servant went to Pada-naram, Rebecca did not disdain to say to him, "Drink, MY LORD," as "she hasted, and let down her pitcher upon her hand, and gave him drink." Laban, the brother of Rebecca, "ungirded his camels, and brought him water to wash his feet, and the men's feet that were with him." In the arrangements of Jacob's household on his journey from Padanaram to Canaan, we find his two maid-servants provided with the same accommodations as Rachel and Leah. Each of them had a separate tent appropriated to her use. Gen. xxxi. 33. The social equality of servants with their masters is an obvious deduction from Ex. xxi. 7, 10, from which we learn that the sale of a young Jewish female as a servant was also her *betrothal as a wife*, either to her master, or to one of his sons. In 1 Sam.

ix. is an account of a festival in the city of Zuph, at
which Samuel presided. None but those bidden sat
at the feast, and only "about thirty persons" were
invited. Quite a select party!—the elite of the city.
Saul and his servant, at Samuel's solicitation, accom-
pany him as invited guests. "And Samuel took Saul
and his SERVANT, and brought THEM into the PARLOR,
(!) and made THEM sit in the CHIEFEST SEATS among
those, that were bidden." A *servant* invited by the
chief judge, ruler, and prophet in Israel, to dine with
a select party, in company with his master, who was
at the same time anointed King of Israel! This was
"*one* of the servants" of Kish, Saul's father; not the
steward or the chief of them; *any* one that could be
most easily spared. David seems to have been for a
time in all respects a servant in Saul's family. "And
Saul sent to Jesse saying, "Let David, I pray thee,
*stand before me.*" He was Saul's personal servant,
went on his errands, played on the harp for his amuse-
ment, bore his armor for him, and when he wished to
visit his parents, asked permission of Jonathan, Saul's
son. Saul also calls him "my servant." 1 Sam. xvi.
21–23; xviii. 5; xx. 5, 6; xxii. 8. Yet David sat
with the king at meat, married his daughter, and lived
on terms of the closest intimacy with the heir appa-
rent. Abimelech, king of Shechem, who afterwards
reigned over all Israel, *was the son of a* MAID-SER-
VANT. His mother's family seems to have been of
note in the city of Shechem, where her brothers held
sway. Judg. ix. 1–6, 18. Jarha, an Egyptian, the
servant of Sheshan, married his daughter. Tobiah,
"the servant," and an Ammonite, married the

daughter of Shecaniah, one of the chief men in Jerusalem, and was the associate of Sanballat, the governor
of the Samaritans.   We find Elah, the King of Israel,
at a festive entertainment in the house of Arza, his
steward, or head-servant.   1 Kings xvi. 8, 9.   See
also the intercourse between Gideon and his servants.
Judg. vi. 27, and vii. 10, 11.   The Levite of Mount
Ephraim and his servant.   Jud. xx. 3, 9, 11, 13, 19,
21, 22.   King Saul and his servant Doeg, one of his
herdmen.   1 Sam. xx. 1, 7; xxii. 9, 18, 22.   King
David and Ziba, the servant of Mephibosheth.   2
Sam. xvi. 1–4.   Jonathan and his servant.   1 Sam.
xiv. 1–14.   Elisha and his servant, Gehazi.   2 Kings
iv. v. vi.   Also between Joram, King of Israel, and
the servant of Elisha.   2 Kings viii. 4, 5, and between Naaman, "the Captain of the host of the king
of Syria," and the same person.   2 Kings v. 21–23.
The fact that servants were invited guests at public
and social festivals, shows also the estimation in
which they were held by the Israelites.

Job "was the greatest man of all the men of the
east."   Job i. 3.   After asserting his integrity, his
justice, and equity, and declaring, "I delivered the
poor," Job adds, "I was eyes to the blind and feet
was I to the lame;" "I was a father to the poor, and
the cause which I knew not I searched out;" * * *
he says, "If I did despise the cause of my man-servant
or my maid-servant when they CONTENDED with me
* * * then let mine arm fall from the shoulder blade."
Job xxix. 12, 15, 16; xxxi. 13, 22.   This is the
phraseology applied in judicial proceedings to those
who implead one another, and shows that Job and his

servants, so far as *rights* are concerned, were equal,
that there was no restraint on their *free speech* in
calling in question his transactions with them, and
that the claims of both parties were adjudicated on
the principle of reciprocal right.  "If I did *despise*
the cause of my man-servant," &c.  In other words,
if I treated it lightly, as though servants had not a
claim for just dues and just estimation as human
beings.  "When they *contended* with me," that is,
when they claimed what was due to them, or ques-
tioned the justice of my dealings with them.

In the context, Job virtually affirms that his servants had the same rights that he had, and were
entitled to equal consideration with himself.  By what
language could he more forcibly utter his conviction
of the identity of their common nature, necessities, and
rights?  He adds, "What then shall I do when God
riseth up? and when he visiteth, what shall I answer
him?  Did not he that made me make *him*? and did
not one fashion us in the womb?"  In the next verse,
Job declares that he has not "*withheld from the
poor their desire.*"  Is it the "desire" of the poor
to be *compelled* to work without *pay*?

III.  THE CASE OF THE GIBEONITES.  The condition
of the inhabitants of Gibeon, under the Hebrew com-
monwealth, is quoted in triumph by the advocates of
slavery.  Milton's devils made desperate snatches at
fruit that turned to ashes on their lips.  The spirit of
slavery raves under torments, and casts about for
something to ease them.  But even the incantations
of the demon cauldron could not extract from this
case enough to tantalize starvation.  What was the

condition of the Gibeonites under the Israelites? 1. *It was voluntary.* Their own proposition to Joshua was to become servants. Josh. ix. 8, 11. It was accepted, but the kind of service was not specified until their gross imposition came to light; they were then assigned to menial offices in the Tabernacle. 2. *They were not domestic servants in the families of the Israelites.* They still resided in their own cities, and exercised the functions of a *distinct,* though dependent community. They were subject to the Jewish nation as *tributaries.* So far from being distributed among the Israelites, they remained a separate community for many centuries. When attacked by the Amorites, they applied to the Israelites for aid—it was rendered, their enemies routed, and themselves left unmolested in their cities. Josh. x. 6–18. Long afterwards, Saul slew some of them, and God sent upon Israel a three years' famine for it. David inquired of the Gibeonites, "What shall I do for you, and wherewith shall I make the atonement?" At their demand he delivered up to them seven of Saul's descendants. 2 Sam. xxi. 1–9. The whole transaction was a recognition of the Gibeonites as a distinct people. There is no intimation that they served either families or individuals of the Israelites, but only the "house of God," or the Tabernacle. This was established first at Gilgal, a day's journey from their cities; and then at Shiloh, nearly two days' journey from them; where it continued about 350 years. During this period, the Gibeonites inhabited their ancient cities and territory. Only a few could have been absent at any time in attendance on the

8

Tabernacle.   Wherever allusion is made to them, the main body are spoken of as *at home*.   It is preposterous to suppose that all the inhabitants of their four cities could find employment at the Tabernacle.   One of them " was a great city, as one of the royal cities ;" so large that a confederacy of five kings was deemed necessary for its destruction.   It is probable that the men were divided into classes, ministering in rotation. As the priests, whose assistants they were, served by courses in rotation a week at a time, it is not improbable that their periods of service were so arranged as to correspond.   This service was their *national tribute* for the privilege of residence and protection under the government.   No service seems to have been required of the *females*.   As these Gibeonites were Canaanites, and as they had greatly exasperated the Israelites by imposition and lying, we might expect that they would reduce *them* to the condition of chattels, if there was *any* case in which God permitted them to do so.

IV. EGYPTIAN BONDAGE ANALYZED.   Throughout the Mosaic system, God warns the Israelites not to hold their servants in such a condition as they were held in by the Egyptians.   How often are they pointed back to the grindings of their prison-house !   What motives to the exercise of justice and kindness towards their servants are held out to their fears in threatened judgments ; to their hopes in promised good ; and to all within them that could feel, by those oft repeated words of tenderness and terror !   " For ye were bondmen in the land of Egypt"—wakening anew the memory of tears and anguish, and of the wrath that avengeth them.   But what was the bondage of the

Israelites in Egypt? Of what rights were they plundered, and what did they retain?

1. *They were not dispersed among the families of Egypt,** but formed a separate community.* Gen. xlvi. 34. Ex. viii. 22, 24; ix. 26; x. 23; xi. 7; iv. 29; ii. 9; xvi. 22; xvii. 5; vi. 14. 2. *They had the exclusive possession of the land of Goshen,†* "*the best part of the land*" *of Egypt.* Gen. xlv. 18; xlvii. 6, 11, 27; Ex. viii. 22; ix. 26; xii. 4. Goshen must have been a considerable distance from those parts of Egypt inhabited by the Egyptians; so far, at least, as to prevent their contact with the Israelites, since the reason assigned for locating them in Goshen was, that shepherds were "an abomination to the Egyptians;" besides, their employments would naturally lead them out of the settled parts of Egypt to find pasturage for their flocks and herds. 3. *They lived in permanent dwellings.* These were *houses*, not *tents*. In Ex. xii. 7, 22, the two side *posts*, and the upper door *posts*, and the lintel of the houses are mentioned. Each family seems to have occupied a house

---

* The Egyptians evidently had *domestic* servants living in their families; these may have been slaves; allusion is made to them in Ex. ix. 14, 20, 21, and xi. 5.

† The land of Goshen was a large tract of country east of the Pelusian arm of the Nile, and between it and the head of the Red Sea, and the lower border of Palestine. The probable centre of that portion, occupied by the Israelites, could hardly have been less than sixty miles from the city. The border of Goshen nearest to Egypt must have been many miles distant. See "Exodus of the Israelites out of Egypt," an able article by Prof. Robinson, in the Biblical Repository for October, 1832.

*by itself.* Acts vii. 20 ; Ex. xii. 4—and judging
from the regulation about the eating of the Passover,
they could hardly have been small ones, Ex. xii. 4 ;
probably contained separate apartments, as the entertainment of sojourners seems to have been a common
usage.   Ex. iii. 23 ; and also places for concealment.
Ex. ii. 2, 3 ; Acts vii. 20.   They appear to have been
well apparelled.   Ex. xii. 11.   4. *They owned "flocks
and herds," and "very much cattle."*   Ex. xii. 4, 6,
32, 37, 38.   From the fact that *"every man"* was
commanded before the people left Egypt, to kill either
a lamb or a kid, one year old, for the Passover, we
infer that even the poorest of the Israelites owned
either sheep or goats.   Further, the multitude of their
flocks and herds may be judged of from the expostula-
tion of Moses with Jehovah.   Num. xii. 21, 22.
" The people among whom I am are six hundred
thousand footmen, and thou hast said, I will give
them flesh that they may eat a whole month ; shall the
flocks and the herds be slain for them to *suffice*
them ?"   As these six hundred thousand were only the
*men* " from twenty years old and upward, that were
able to go forth to war," Ex. i. 45, 46, the whole
number of the Israelites could not have been less than
three million and a half.   Flocks and herds to
" suffice" all these for food might surely be called
" very much cattle."   5. *They had their own form
of government,* and preserved their tribe and family
divisions, and their internal organization throughout,
though still a province of Egypt, and *tributary* to it.
Ex. ii. 1 ; xii. 19, 21 ; vi. 14, 25 ; v. 19 ; iii. 16, 18.
6. *They had, in a considerable degree, the disposal*

*of their own time.* Ex. iii. 16, 18; xii. 6; ii. 9; and
iv. 27, 29–31. *They seem to have practised some of
the fine arts.* Ex. xxxii. 4; xxxv. 22, 35. 7. *They
were all armed.* Ex. xxxii. 27. 8. *They held their
possessions independently, and the Egyptians seem
to have regarded them as inviolable.* No intimation is given that the Egyptians dispossessed them of
their habitations, or took away their flocks, or herds,
or crops, or implements of agriculture, or any article
of property. 9. *The females seem to have known
something of domestic refinements.* They were
familiar with instruments of music, and skilled in the
working of fine fabrics. Ex. xv. 20; xxxv. 25, 26;
and both males and females were able to read and
write. Deut. xi. 18–20; xvii. 19; xxvii. 3. 10.
*Service seems to have been exacted from none but
adult males.* Nothing is said from which the bond-
service of females could be inferred; the hiding of
Moses three months by his mother, and the payment
of wages to her by Pharaoh's daughter, go against
such a supposition. Ex. ii. 29. 11. *Their food
was abundant, and of great variety.* So far from
being fed upon a fixed allowance of a single article,
and hastily prepared, "they sat by the flesh-pots," and
"did eat bread to the full." Ex. xvi. 3; and their
bread was prepared with leaven. Ex. xii. 15, 39.
They ate "the fish freely, the cucumbers, and the
melons, and the leeks, and the onions, and the garlic."
Num. xi. 4, 5; xx. 5. Probably but a small portion
of the people were in the service of the Egyptians at
any one time. The extent and variety of their possessions, together with such cultivation of their crops

as would provide them with bread, and such care of
their flocks and herds as would secure their profitable
increase, must have kept at home the main body of the
nation. During the plague of darkness, " ALL the
children of Israel had light in their dwellings." We
infer that they were *there* to enjoy it. See also Ex.
ix. 26. It seems improbable that the making of brick,
the only service named during the latter part of their
sojourn in Egypt, could have furnished permanent
employment for the bulk of the nation. See also Ex.
iv. 29–31. Besides, when Eastern nations employed
tributaries, it was as now, in the use of the levy,
requiring them to furnish a given quota, drafted off
periodically, so that comparatively but a small portion
of the nation would be absent *at any one time.* The
adult males of the Israelites were probably divided
into companies, which relieved each other at stated
intervals of weeks or months. It might have been
during one of these periodical furloughs from service
that Aaron performed the journey to Horeb. Ex.
iv. 27. At the least calculation, this journey must
have consumed *eight weeks.* Probably one-fifth part
of the proceeds of their labor was required of the
Israelites, in common with the Egyptians. Gen.
xlvii. 24, 26. Instead of taking it from their *crops*
(Goshen being better for *pasturage*), they exacted
it of them in brick making ; and labor might have
been exacted only from the *poorer* Israelites, the
wealthy being able to pay their tribute in money.
The fact that all the elders of Israel seem to have
controlled their own time (see Ex. iv. 29 ; iii. 16 ; v.
20), favors the supposition. Ex. iv. 27, 31. Con-

trast this bondage of Egypt with American slavery.
Have our slaves "flocks and herds, even very much
cattle ?" Do they live in commodious houses of their
own, "sit by the flesh-pots," "eat fish freely," and
"eat bread to the full ?" Do they live in a separate
community, in their distinct tribes, under their own
rulers, in the exclusive occupation of an extensive
tract of country for the culture of their crops, and for
rearing immense herds of their own cattle—and all
these held inviolable by their masters ? Are our
female slaves free from exactions of labor and liabilities of outrage ? or, when employed, are they paid
wages, as was the Israelitish woman by the king's
daughter ? Have they the disposal of their own time,
and the means of cultivating social refinements, and
for personal improvement ? THE ISRAELITES, UNDER
THE BONDAGE OF EGYPT, ENJOYED ALL THESE RIGHTS
AND PRIVILEGES. True, "all the service wherein
they made them serve was with rigor." But what
was this when compared with the incessant toil of
American slaves ; the robbery of all their time and
earnings, and even the "power to own anything, or
acquire anything ?" a "quart of corn a day," the legal
allowance of food !* their *only* clothing for one-half
the year, "*one* shirt and *one* pair of pantaloons !"†
their dwellings, *hovels*, unfit for human residence, with
but one apartment, where both sexes and all ages herd
promiscuously at night, like the beasts of the field.
Add to this the ignorance and degradation, the daily

---

* See law of North Carolina, Haywood's Manual, 524–5.
† See law of Louisiana, Martin's Digest, 6, 10.

sunderings of kindred, the revelries of lust, the lacera-
tions and baptisms of blood, sanctioned by law, and
patronized by public sentiment.    What was the bondage of Egypt when compared with this?    And yet
for her oppression of the poor, God smote her with
plagues, and trampled her as the mire, till she passed
away in his wrath, and the place that knew her in her
pride knew her no more.    Ah!  "I have seen the
afflictions of my people, and I have heard their groan-
ings, and am come down to deliver them."    HE DID
COME, and Egypt sank a ruinous heap, and her blood
closed over her.    If such was God's retribution for the
oppressions of heathen Egypt, of how much sorer
punishment shall a Christian people be thought
worthy, who cloak with religion a system, in compari-
son with which the bondage of Egypt dwindles to
nothing?    Did God commission his people to rob
others of *all* their rights, while he denounced against
them wrath to the uttermost, if they practised the *far
lighter* oppression of Egypt—which robbed them of
only the least of their rights, and left the females
unplundered even of these?    Is God divided against
himself?    When He had just turned Egypt into a
funeral pile;  while his curse yet blazed upon her
unburied dead, and his bolts still hissed amidst her
slaughter, and the smoke of her torment went upward
because she had "ROBBED THE POOR," did He license
the VICTIMS of robbery to rob the poor of ALL ?    As
*Lawgiver*, did he *create* a system tenfold more grind-
ing than that for which he had just hurled Pharaoh
headlong, and overwhelmed his princes and his hosts,
till " hell was moved to meet them at their coming !"

We now examine various objections set in array against these conclusions.

## OBJECTIONS CONSIDERED.

The advocates of slavery are at their wit's end in pressing the Bible into their service. Their ever-varying shifts and forced constructions proclaim both their *cause* desperate, and themselves. Meanwhile, their invocations for help to "those good old slaveholders and patriarchs, Abraham, Isaac, and Jacob,"* avail

---

* The Presbytery of Harmony, South Carolina, at their meeting in Wainsborough, S. C., Oct. 28, 1836, appointed a special committee to report on slavery. The following resolution is a part of the report adopted by the Presbytery.

"Resolved, That slavery has existed from the days of those GOOD OLD SLAVEHOLDERS AND PATRIARCHS, Abraham, Isaac, and Jacob, who are now in the kingdom of Heaven."

Abraham receives abundant honor at the hands of slaveholding divines. Not because he was the "father of the faithful," and forsook home and country for the truth's sake, for all this he gets faint praise ; but then he had " SERVANTS BOUGHT WITH MONEY ! ! !" This is the finishing touch of his character. Prose fledges into poetry, eulogy rarifies into panegyric, and goes off in rhapsody. In their ecstasies over Abraham, Isaac's paramount claims are lost sight of. No slaveholder casts loving glances at Gen. xxvii. 29, 37, where Isaac, addressing Jacob, says, "Be *lord* over thy brethren, and let thy mother's sons *bow down* to thee." And afterwards, addressing Esau, he says, speaking of the birth-right immunities confirmed to Jacob, "Behold, I have made him thy *lord*, and all his brethren have I GIVEN TO HIM FOR SERVANTS."

Here is a " Divine Warrant" for a father holding his *children*

as little as did the screams of Baal's prophets to bring
an answer of fire.   The Bible defences thrown around
slavery by professed ministers of the Gospel do so torture common sense, Scripture, and historical facts, it
were hard to tell whether absurdity, fatuity, ignorance
or blasphemy predominates, in the compound.   How
often has it been bruited that the color of the negro is
the *Cain-mark!*   Cain's posterity started an opposi-

---

as slaves, and bequeathing them to his heirs!   Better still, it
proves that the practice of slaveholders in bequeathing their
*colored* children to those of a different hue, was a "Divine
institution;" for Isaac " *gave*" Esau, who was " *red* all over," to
Jacob, " *as a servant.*"   Now, gentlemen, "honor to whom
honor."   Let Isaac no longer be stinted of his glory as your
great prototype in that nice discrimination, by which a father
makes part of his children *property*, and the rest their *pro-
prietors*, whenever duty is made plain by the decisive tokens
of COLOR and HAIR (for, to show that Esau was Jacob's *rightful*
property the difference in *hair*, as well as color, is stated by
inspiration).

One patriarchal example is quite overlooked by slaveholders.   Isaac informs Jacob that those "given to him as
servants" were " HIS BRETHREN" (twice repeated).   True, it
would be an odd codicil to a will for a slaveholder, after
bequeathing to *some* of his children all his slaves, to inform
them that certain of them were their *brothers and sisters.*   It
might be at first a sore trial; but what *pious* slaveholder
would not follow thus in the footsteps of his patriarchal predecessors!

Great reformers must make great sacrifices; and if the
world is to be brought back to the purity of patriarchal
times, to whom will all failing eyes turn, if not to slaveholders, who have reproduced the "patriarchal institution"
of *concubinage*, and faithfully stamped their own image in
variegated hues, upon a swarming progeny!

tion to the ark, forsooth, and rode out the flood with flying streamers ! How could miracle better vindicate the ways of God to man, than by pointing such an argument, and filling out for slaveholders a Divine title-deed !

OBJECTION 1. *"Cursed be Canaan, a servant of servants shall he be unto his brethren."* Gen. ix. 25.

This prophecy of Noah is the *vade mecum* of slaveholders, and they never venture abroad without it; it is a pocket-piece for sudden occasion, a keepsake to dote over, a charm to spell-bind opposition, and a magnet to draw to their standard " whatsoever worketh abomination or maketh a lie." Yet "cursed be Canaan" is but a mocking lullaby to unquiet tossings. Those who justify negro slavery by the curse on Canaan *assume*, as usual, all the points in debate. 1. That *slavery* was prophesied, rather than mere *service* to others, and *individual* bondage rather than *national* subjection and tribute. 2. That the *prediction* of crime justifies it; or, at least, absolves those whose crimes fulfil it. How piously the Pharaohs might have quoted the prophecy, " *Thy seed shall be a stranger in a land that is not theirs, and they shall afflict them four hundred years !*" And then, what saints were those that crucified the Lord of glory ! 3. That the Africans are descendants from Canaan. Africa was peopled from Egypt and Ethiopia, which were settled by Mizraim and Cush. For the location and boundaries of Canaan's posterity, see Gen. x. 15– 19. So a prophecy of evil to one people, is quoted to justify its infliction upon another. Perhaps it may be argued that Canaan includes all Ham's posterity. If

so, the prophecy is yet unfulfilled. The other sons
of Ham settled Egypt and Assyria, and, conjointly
with Shem, Persia, and to some extent, the Grecian
and Roman empires. The history of these nations
gives no verification of the prophecy. Whereas, the
history of Canaan's descendants, for more than three
thousand years, is a record of its fulfilment. First,
they were put to tribute by the Israelites; then by the
Medes and Persians; then by the Macedonians,
Grecians, and Romans, successively; and finally, by
the Ottoman dynasty, under which they yet remain.
Thus Canaan has been for ages the servant mainly of
Shem and Japhet, and secondarily of the other sons
of Ham. It may still be objected, that though Canaan
alone is *named*, yet that the 22d and 24th verses show
the posterity of Ham in general to be meant. "And
Ham, the father of Canaan, saw the nakedness of his
father, and told his two brethren without." "And
Noah awoke from his wine, and knew what his
YOUNGER son had done unto him, and said," &c. It
is argued that this "*younger* son" cannot be *Canaan*,
as he was the *grandson* of Noah, and therefore it
must be *Ham*. We answer, whoever that "*younger
son*" was, *Canaan* alone was named in the prophecy.
Besides, the Hebrew word *Ben* signifies son, grandson, or *any one* of the posterity of an individual.*
"*Know ye Laban the* SON (grandson) *of Nahor?*"
Gen. xxix. 5. "*Mephibosheth, the* SON (grandson) *of*

* So *äv*, the Hebrew word for father, signifies any ancestor,
however remote. 2 Chron. xvii. 3; xxviii. 1; xxxiv. 2,
Dan. v. 2.

*Saul.*" 2 Sam. xix. 24; 2 Sam. ix. 6. "*The driving of Jehu, the* SON (grandson) *of Nimshi.*" 2 Kings ix. 20. See also Ruth iv. 17; 2 Sam. xxi. 6; Gen. xxxi. 55. Further, Ham was not the "*younger* son." The order of enumeration makes him the *second* son. If it be said that Bible usage varies, the order of birth not always being observed; the reply is, that enumeration in that order is the *rule*, in any other order the *exception*. Besides, if a younger member of a family takes precedence of older ones in the family record, it is a mark of pre-eminence, either in endowments or providential instrumentality. Abraham, though sixty years younger than his eldest brother, stands first in the family genealogy. Nothing in Ham's history shows him pre-eminent; besides, the Hebrew word *hăkkātān*, rendered "the *younger*," means *little, small*. The same word is used in Isa. lx. 22. "A LITTLE ONE *shall become a thousand.*" Isa. xxii. 24. "*All vessels of* SMALL *quantity.*" Ps. cxv. 13. "*He will bless them that fear the Lord both* SMALL *and great.*" Ex. xviii. 22. "*But every* SMALL *matter they shall judge.*" It would be a literal rendering of Gen. ix. 24, if it were translated thus, "When Noah knew what his little son,"* or grandson (*Běno hăkkātān*) "had done unto him, he said, Cursed be Canaan," &c. Further, even if the Africans were the descendants of Canaan, the assumption that their enslavement fulfils this prophecy lacks even plausibility; for, only a *fraction* of the inhabitants of Africa have at any time

---

* The French follows the same analogy; *grandson* being *petit fils* (little son).

been the slaves of other nations.   If the objector say,
in reply, that a majority of the Africans have always
been slaves *at home,* we answer : *It is false in point
of fact;* but *if it were true,* how does it help the
argument ?   The prophecy was, " Cursed be Canaan,
a servant of servants shall he be *unto his* BRETHREN,"
not unto *himself!*

OBJECTION II.—"*If a man smite his servant or
his maid with a rod, and he die under his hand,
he shall surely be punished.   Notwithstanding, if he
continue a day or two, he shall not be punished, for
he is his money.*" Ex. xxi. 20, 21.   What was the
design of this regulation !   Was it to grant masters
an indulgence to beat servants with impunity, and an
assurance that, if they beat them to death, the offence
should not be *capital?*   This is substantially what
proslavery commentators tell us.   What Diety do
such men worship ?   Some blood-gorged Moloch,
enthroned on human hecatombs ?   Did He who thun-
dered from Sinai, "THOU SHALT NOT KILL," offer a
bounty on *murder?*   Whoever analyzes the Mosaic
system will often find a moot court in session, trying
law points, settling definitions, or laying down rules
of  evidence.   Num. xxxv. 10–22 ; Deut. xix. 4–6 ;
Lev. xxiv. 19–22 ; Ex. xxi. 18, 19, are some of the
cases stated, with tests furnished the judges by which
to detect *the intent,* in actions brought before them.
The detail gone into is to enable them to get at the
*motive,* and find out whether the master *designed* to
kill.   1.  " If a man smite his servant with a *rod.*"
The instrument used, gives a clue to the *intent.*   See
Num. xxxv. 16. 18.   A *rod,* not an axe, nor a sword,

nor a bludgeon, nor any other death-weapon; hence, from the *kind* of instrument, no design to *kill* would be inferred; for *intent* to kill would hardly have taken a *rod* for its weapon. But if the servant "*die under his hand*," then the unfitness of the instrument is point blank against him; for, striking with a *rod* so as to cause death presupposes many blows and great violence, and these kept up till the death-gasp, showed an *intent to kill*. Hence, "he shall *surely* be punished." But if he continued a day or two, the *length of time that he lived*, the *kind* of instrument used, and .the master's pecuniary interest in his *life*, ("he is his *money*"), all made a strong case of presumptive evidence, that the master did not *design to* kill. Further the word *năkăm*, here rendered *punished*, occurs thirty-five times in the Old Testament, and in almost every place is translated "*avenge*," in a few, "*to take vengeance*," or "*to revenge*," and in this instance ALONE "*punish*." As it stands in our translation, the pronoun preceding it refers to the *master;* whereas it should refer to the *crime*, and the word rendered *punished* should have been rendered *avenged*. The meaning is this : If a man smite his servant or his maid with a rod, and he die under his hand, IT (the death) shall surely be avenged, or, literally, *by avenging it shall be avenged;* that is, the *death* of the servant shall be *avenged* by the *death* of the master. So "If he continue a day or two," his death is not to be avenged by the *death* of the *master*, as in that case the crime was to be adjudged *man-slaughter*, and not *murder*. In the following verse, another case of personal injury is stated, for which the injurer is to pay *a sum of money;* and yet our translators employ the same phraseology in both places! One, an instance of deliberate, wanton, killing by piecemeal; the other, an accidental injury. Of the inflictor, in both cases, they say the same thing! Now, just the discrimination to be looked for where GOD legislates is marked in the original. In the case of the servant wilfully murdered, He says, "It (the death) shall surely be *avenged,*"—that is, the life of the wrong-doer shall expiate the crime. The same word is used in the Old Testament, when the greatest wrongs are redressed by devoting the perpetrators to *destruction.* In the case of the unintentional injury, in the following verse, God says, "he shall surely be *fined* (*ānăsh*). "He shall *pay* as the judges determine." The simple meaning of the word *ānăsh* is to lay a fine. It is used in Deut. xxii. 19: "They shall *amerce* him in one hundred shekels," and in 2 Chron. xxxvi. 3: "He condemned (*mulcted*) the land in a hundred talents of silver and a talent of gold." That *avenging* the death of the servant was neither imprisonment, nor stripes, nor a fine, but that it was *taking the master's life,* we infer, 1. From the *use* of the word *nākăm.* See Gen. iv. 24; Josh. x. 13; Judg. xv. 7; xvi. 28; 1 Sam. xiv. 24; xviii. 25; xxv. 31; 2 Sam. iv. 8; Judg. v. 2; 1 Sam. xxv. 26–33. 2. From the express statute, Lev. xxiv. 17: "He that killeth ANY man shall surely be put to death." Also, Num. xxv. 30, 31: "Whoso killeth ANY person, the murderer shall be put to death. Moreover, ye shall take NO SATISFACTION for the life of a murderer which is guilty of death, but he shall surely

be put to death." 3. The Targum of Jonathan gives
the verse thus, "Death by the sword shall surely be
adjudged." The Targum of Jerusalem, "Vengeance
shall be taken for him to the *uttermost.*" Jarchi, the
same. The Samaritan version : "He shall die the
death." Again, "for he is his money," is quoted to
prove that the servant is his master's property, and
therefore if he died, the master was not to be punished.
The assumption is, that the clause proves not only
that the servant is *worth money* to the master, but
that he is an *article of property.* If the advocates
of slavery will take this principle of interpretation
into the Bible, and turn it loose, let them stand and
draw in self-defence. If they indorse it at one point,
they must stand sponsors all around the circle. It
will be too late to cry for quarter when its stroke
clears the table, and tilts them among the sweepings
beneath. The Bible abounds with such expressions
as the following : "This (bread) *is* my body ;" "all
they (the Israelites) *are* brass and tin ;" "this
(water) *is* the blood of the men who went in jeopardy
of their lives ;" "the Lord God *is* a sun ;" "the seven
good ears *are* seven years ;". "the tree of the field *is*
man's life ;" "God *is* a consuming fire ;" "he *is* his
money," &c. The words of the original are (*Kāspo-
hu*), "his *silver* is he." The objector's principle of
interpretation is a philosopher's stone ! It transmutes
five feet eight inches of flesh and bones into *solid
silver!* Quite a *permanent* servant, if not so nimble
withal ! The obvious meaning of the phrase, "*He is
his money,*" is, he is *worth money* to his master ; and

9*

since, if the master had killed him, it would have taken money out of his pocket, the *pecuniary loss*, the *kind of instrument used*, and *the fact of his living some time after the injury* (if the master *meant* to kill, he would be likely to *do* it while about it), altogether make a strong case of presumptive evidence clearing the master from *intent to kill*. But let us look at the objector's *inferences*. One is, that as the master might dispose of his *property* as he pleased, he was not to be punished, if he destroyed it. Whether the servant died under the master's hand, or after a day or two, he was *equally* his property ; and the objector admits that, in the *first* case, the master is to be "surely punished" for destroying *his own property !* The other inference is, that since the continuance of a day or two cleared the master of *intent to kill*, the loss of the servant would be a sufficient punishment for inflicting the injury which caused his death. This inference makes the Mosaic law false to its own principles. A *pecuniary loss* was no part of the legal claim where a person took the *life* of another. In such case, the law spurned money, whatever the sum. God would not cheapen human life by balancing it with such a weight. "Ye shall take NO SATISFACTION for the life of a murderer, but he shall surely be put to death." Num. xxxv. 31. Even in excusable homicide, where an axe slipped from the helve and killed a man, no sum of money availed to release from confinement in the city of refuge, until the death of the High Priest. Num. xxxv. 32. The doctrine that the loss of the servant would be a penalty *adequate* to the desert of the master, admits

his *guilt* and his desert of *some* punishment, and it
prescribes a kind of punishment, rejected by the law,
in all cases where man took the life of man, whether
with or without intent to kill.   In short the objector
annuls an integral part of the system—makes a *new*
law, and coolly metes out such penalty as he thinks fit.
The master who struck out his servant's tooth, whether
intentionally or not, was required to set him free.   The
*pecuniary loss* to the master was the same as though
he had killed him.   Contrast the two cases.   A master
beats his servant, so that he dies ; another accidentally
strikes out his servant's tooth ; *the pecuniary loss of
both masters is the same.*   If the loss of the servant's
services is punishment sufficient for the crime of killing him, would *God* command the same punishment
for the accidental knocking out of a *tooth?*   Indeed,
unless the injury were done *inadvertently*, the loss of
the servant's services was only a part of the punishment—mere reparation to the *individual* for injury
done ; the main punishment, that strictly *judicial*, was
reparation to the *community*.   To set the servant
*free*, and thus proclaim his injury, his right to redress,
and the measure of it, answer not the ends of *public*
justice.   The law made an example of the offender,
that "those that remain might hear and fear."   "If a
man cause a blemish in his neighbor, as he hath done,
so shall it be done unto him.   Breach for breach, eye
for eye, tooth for tooth.   Ye shall have one manner
of law as well for the STRANGER as for one of your
own country."   Lev. xxiv. 19, 20, 22.   Finally, if a
master smote out *his* servant's tooth, the law smote
out his tooth—thus redressing the *public* wrong ; and

it cancelled the servant's obligation to the master, thus
giving some compensation for the injury done, and
exempting him from perilous liabilities in future.

OBJECTION III. "*Both thy bondmen and thy bondmaids which thou shalt have, shall be of the heathen
that are round about you; of them shall ye buy
bondmen and bondmaids. Moreover, of the children
of the strangers that do sojourn among you, of them
shall ye buy, and of their families that are with you,
which they begat in your land, and they shall be your
possession. And ye shall take them as an inheritance
for your children after you, to inherit them for a
possession; they shall be your bondmen forever.*"
. Lev. xxv. 44–46.

The *points* in these verses, urged as proof that the
Mosaic system sanctioned slavery, are, 1. The word
"BONDMEN." 2. "BUY." 3. "INHERITANCE AND
POSSESSION." 4. "FOREVER."

1. "BONDMEN." The fact that servants from the
heathen are called "*bondmen*," while others are called
"*servants*" is quoted as proof that the former were
slaves. As the caprices of King James's translators
were not inspired, we need stand in no special awe
of them. The word here rendered bondmen is uniformly rendered servants elsewhere. The Hebrew
word "*ĕbĕdh*," the plural of which is here translated
"*bondmen*," is often applied to Christ. "Behold my
*servant* (bondman, slave?) whom I uphold." Isa.
xlii. 1. "Behold my *servant* (Christ) shall deal
prudently." Isa. lii. 13. "And he said, it is a light
thing that thou (Christ) shouldst be my *servant*."
Isa. xlix. 6. "To a *servant* of rulers." Isa. xlix. 7.

"By his knowledge shall my righteous *servant*
(Christ) justify many." Is. liii. 11. "Behold, I will
bring forth my *servant*, the BRANCH." Zech. iii. 8.
In 1 Kings, xii. 6, 7, it is applied to King Rehoboam.
"And they spake unto him, saying, if thou wilt be a
*servant* unto this people, then they will be thy *servants* forever." In 2 Chron. xii. 7, 8, 9, 13, it is
applied to the king and all the nation. The word is
used to designate those who perform service for
*individuals or families*, about thirty-five times in the
Old Testament. To designate *tributaries*, about
twenty-five times. To designate the *subjects of
government*, about thirty-three times. To designate
worshippers both of the true God, and of false gods,
about seventy times. It is also used in salutations
and courteous addresses nearly one hundred times.
In fine, the word is applied to all persons doing
service for others, and that *merely to designate them
as the performers of such service*, whatever it might
be, or whatever the ground on which it might be
rendered. To argue from the fact of this word being
used to designate domestic servants, that they were
made servants by *force*, worked without pay, and were
held as articles of property, is such a gross assumption and absurdity as to make formal refutation ridi-
culous. We repeat that the word rendered bondmen
in Lev. xxv. 44, is used to point out persons rendering service irrespective of the principle on which that
service was rendered. It is applied indiscriminately
to tributaries, to domestics, to all the subjects of
governments, to magistrates, to all governmental
officers, to younger sons—defining their relation to the

first-born, who is called *lord* and *ruler*—to prophets, to kings, and to the Messiah. To argue, that those to whom the word *ēbĕdh* was applied rendered service against their wills and without pay, does violence to the Scripture use of the term, sets at nought all rules of interpretation, and outrages common sense. If *any* inference as to the meaning of the term is to be drawn from the relations of the various classes of persons, to whom it is applied, the legitimate one would seem to be, that the term designates a person who renders service to another in return for value received. The same remark applies to the Hebrew verb *ăbădh*, to serve. It is used in the Old Testament to describe the *serving* of tributaries, of worshippers, of domestics, of Levites, of sons to a father, of younger brothers to the elder, of subjects to a ruler, of hirelings, of soldiers, of public officers to the government, of a host to his guests, &c. Of these it is used to describe the serving of *worshippers* more than forty times, of *tributaries*, about thirty-five, and of servants or domestics, about *ten*.

If the Israelites not only held slaves, but multitudes of them, if Abraham had thousands, and if they abounded under the Mosaic system, why had their language no word that *meant slave?* That language must be poverty-stricken which has no signs for the most familiar objects and conditions. To represent by the same word property, and the owner of that property, is a solecism. Ziba was an *"ēbĕdh,"* yet he *"owned"* (!) twenty *ēbĕdhs!* In our language, we have both *servant* and *slave*. Why? Because we have both the *things*, and need *signs* for them. If the tongue had a sheath, as swords have scabbard's, we should have some *name* for it : but our dictionaries give us none.    Why?    Because there is no such *thing*.    But the objector asks, " Would not the Israelites use their word *ĕbĕdh*, if they spoke of the slave of a heathen ?"    Answer.    Their *national* servants, or tributaries, are spoken of frequently, but domestic servants so rarely that no necessity existed, even if they were slaves, for coining a new word.    Besides, the fact of their being domestics, under *heathen laws and usages*, proclaimed their liabilities ; their *locality* made a *specific* term unnecessary.    But if the Israelites had not only *servants*, but a multitude of *slaves*, a *word meaning slave* would have been indispensable.    Further, the laws of the Mosaic system were so many sentinels on the outposts to warn off foreign practices.    The border ground of Canaan was quarantine ground, enforcing the strictest non-intercourse in usages between the without and the within.

2. " Buy."    The *buying* of servants is discussed at length. pp. 17–23.    We will add but a single consideration.    This regulation, requiring the Israelites to " *buy*" servants of the heathen, prohibited their taking them without buying.    *Buying* supposes two parties, a *price* demanded by one and paid by the other, and, consequently, the *consent* of both buyer and seller to the transaction.    Of course, the command to the Israelites to *buy* servants of the heathen prohibited their getting them, unless they first got *somebody's* consent to the transaction, and paid to *somebody* a fair equivalent.    Who were these *some-*

*bodies?* Were they the persons themselves who became servants, or some *other* persons ? "Some *other* persons, to be sure," says the objector, "the countrymen
or the neighbors of those who became servants." Ah!
this, then, is the import of the Divine command to the
Israelites : "When you go among the heathen to get
a man to work for you, I straitly charge you to go
first to his *neighbors*, get *their* consent, settle the terms
with *them*, and pay them a fair equivalent.   Then you
may catch the man and drag him home with you; and
I will bless you in the work of your hands.   As to
the man himself, his choice is nothing, and you need
give him nothing for his work : but take care and pay
his *neighbors* well for him, and respect *their* free
choice in taking him—for to deprive a heathen man
by force, and without pay of the *use of himself*, is
well-pleasing in my sight; but to deprive his heathen
neighbors of the use of him is that abominable thing
which my soul hateth."

3. "FOREVER."   This is quoted to prove that
servants were to serve during their lifetime, and
their posterity from generation to generation.*   The
word "forever," instead of defining the length of *individual* service, proclaims the permanence of the regulation laid down in the two verses preceding, namely,
that their *permanent domestics* should be of the
*strangers*, and not of the Israelites; it declares the
duration of that general provision.   As if God had

---

* One would think that the explicit testimony of our Lord
should forever forestall all cavil on this point.  "*The servant
abideth not in the house*, FOREVER, but the Son, abideth ever."
John viii. 35.

said, "You shall *always* get your *permanent* laborers from the nations round about you; your servants shall *always* be of that class of persons." As it stands in the original, it is plain—"*Forever of them shall ye serve yourselves.*" This is the literal rendering.

That "*forever*" refers to the permanent relations of a *community*, rather than to the services of *individuals*, is a fair inference from the form of the expression, "Both thy bondmen, &c., shall be of the *heathen*. OF THEM shall ye buy." "THEY shall be your possession." "THEY shall be your bondmen forever." "But over your brethren, the CHILDREN OF ISRAEL," &c. The language used applies more naturally to a *body* of people, than to *individual* servants. Besides, *perpetual* service cannot be argued from the term *forever*. The ninth and tenth verses of the same chapter limit it absolutely by the jubilee. "Then thou shalt cause the trumpet of the jubilee to sound  *  *  throughout ALL your land." "And ye shall proclaim liberty throughout all the land unto ALL the inhabitants thereof." It may be objected that "inhabitants" here means *Israelitish* inhabitants. In the sixth verse, there is an enumeration of the different classes of the inhabitants, in which servants and strangers are included; and in all the regulations of the jubilee and the sabbatical year, the strangers are included in the precepts, prohibitions, and promises. Again: the year of jubilee was ushered in by the day of atonement. What did these institutions show forth? The day of atonement prefigured the atonement of Christ, and the year of jubilee, the gospel jubilee. And did they prefigure an atonement

10

and a jubilee to *Jews* only ? Were they types of sin
remitted, and of salvation proclaimed to *Israel* alone ?
Is there no redemption for us Gentiles in these ends
of the earth, and is our hope presumption and impiety ?
Did that old partition wall survive the shock that
made earth quake, and hid the sun, burst graves and
rocks, and rent the temple veil ? and did the Gospel
only rear it higher to thunder direr perdition from its
frowning battlements on all without ?

To deny that the blessings of the jubilee extended
to the servants from the *Gentiles* makes Christianity
*Judaism.** It not only eclipses the glory of the Gospel, but strikes out its sun. The refusal to release
servants at the jubilee falsified and disannulled a
grand leading type of the atonement, and was a libel
on the doctrine of Christ's redemption. But, even if
*forever* did refer to *individual* service, we have
ample precedents for limiting the term by the jubilee.
The same word defines the length of time which *Jewish* servants served who did not go out .at the end of

---

* So far from the strangers not being released by the proclamation of liberty on the morning of the jubilee, they were
the only persons who were, *as a body*, released by it. The
rule regulating the service of the Hebrew servant was, "Six
years shall he serve, and in the seventh year he shall go out
free." The *freeholders* who had "fallen into decay," and had
in consequence mortgaged their possessions to their more
prosperous neighbors, and become in some sort their servants;
were released by the jubilee, and again resumed their inheritances. This was the only class of Jewish servants which
was released by the jubilee; all others went out at the close
of their six years' term.

their six years' term. And all admit that they went
out at the jubilee. Ex. xxi. 2–6; Deut. xv. 12–17.
The 23d verse of the same chapter is quoted to prove
that "*forever*" in the 46th verse extends beyond the
jubilee. " The land shall not be sold FOREVER, for
the land is mine." As *forever*, in the 46th verse,
respects the *general arrangement*, and not *individual
service*, the objection does not touch the argument.
Besides, in the 46th verse, the word used is *Olam*,
meaning *throughout the period*, whatever that may
be; whereas in the 23d verse it is *Tsemithuth*, meaning, *a cutting off*, or *to be cut off;* and the import
of it is, that the owner of an inheritance shall not
forfeit his *proprietorship* of it; though it may for a
time pass from his control into the hands of his
creditors or others, yet the owner shall be permitted
to *redeem* it, and even if that be not done, it shall not
be " *cut off*," but shall revert to him at the jubilee.

4. " INHERITANCE AND POSSESSION." " Ye shall
take them as an INHERITANCE for your children after
you, to inherit them for a POSSESSION. This refers to
the *nations*, and not to the *individual* servants procured from these nations. The holding of servants as
a *possession* is discussed at large, pp. 73–92. To
what is there advanced, we here subjoin a few considerations. We have already shown that servants
could not be held as a *property*-possession and inheritance; that they became such of their *own accord*,
were paid wages, released from their regular labor
nearly *half the days in each year, instructed* and
*protected* in all their personal, social, and religious
rights, equally with their masters. All remaining,

after these reservations, would be small temptation,
either to the lust of power or of lucre. What if our
American slaves were all placed in *just such a condition!* Alas, for that melodious circumlocution,
"OUR PECULIAR species of property!" Verily, empha-
sis would be cadence, and euphony and irony meet
together! What eager snatches at mere words and
bald technics, irrespective of connection, principles of
construction, biblical usage, or limitations of meaning
by other passages—and all to eke out such a sense as
sanctifies existing usages!! The words *nahal* and
*nahala,* inherit and inheritance, by no means necessarily signify *articles of property.* "The people
answered the king and said, We have none *inheritance* in the son of Jesse." 2 Chron. x. 16. Did
they mean gravely to disclaim the holding of their
king as an article of *property?* "Children are an
*heritage* (inheritance) of the Lord." Ps. cxxvii. 3.
"Pardon our iniquity, and take us for thine *inheritance.*" Ex. xxxiv. 9. When God pardons his
enemies, and adopts them as children, does he make
them *articles of property?* Are forgiveness and
chattel-making synonymes? "*I* am their *inheritance.*" Ezek. xliv. 28. "I shall give thee the
heathen for thine *inheritance.*" Ps. ii. 18. See also
Deut. iv. 20; Josh. xiii. 33; Ps. lxxxii. 8; lxxviii.
62, 71; Prov. xiv. 18.

The question whether the servants were a PRO-
PERTY-"*possession*" has been already discussed, pp.
73–92; we need add but a word. As an illustration
of the condition of servants from the heathen that were
the "possession" of Israelitish families, and of the way

in which they became servants, see Isa. xiv. 1, 2.
"For the Lord will have mercy on Jacob, and will
yet choose Israel, and set them in their own land;
and the strangers will be *joined* with them, and *they*
*shall* CLEAVE *to the house of Jacob.* And the
people shall take them, and bring them to their place,
and the house of Israel shall *possess* them in the land
of the Lord for servants and handmaids; and they
shall take them captives whose captives they were;
and they shall rule over their oppressors."

We learn from these verses, 1st. That these servants
which were to be "*possessed*" by the Israelites, were
to be "joined with them," *i. e.*, become proselytes to
their religion.   2d. That they should " CLEAVE to the
house of Jacob," *i. e.*, that they would forsake their
own people voluntarily, attach themselves to the
Israelites as servants, and of their own choice accom-
pany them on their return, as Ruth accompanied
Naomi from Moab to the land of Israel; and as the
"souls gotten" by Abraham in Padanaram, accompanied him when he went to Canaan.   "And the
house of Israel shall *possess* them for servants," *i. e.*,
shall *have* them for servants.

In the passage under consideration, "they shall be
your *possession*," the original word translated "possession" is *ahuzza*.   The same word is used in Gen.
xlvii. 11.   "And Joseph placed his father and his
brethren, and gave them a *possession* in the land of
Egypt." Gen. xlvii. 11.   In what sense was Goshen
the *possession* of the Israelites?   Answer, in the
sense of *having it to live in*, not in the sense of
having it as *owners*.   In what sense were the Israel-

10*

ites to *possess* these nations, and *take them* as an *inheritance for their children?* Answer, they possessed them as a permanent source of supply for household servants. And this relation to these nations was to go down to posterity as a standing regulation, having the certainty and regularity of a descent by inheritance. The sense of the whole regulation may be given thus: "Thy permanent domestics, which thou shalt have, shall be of the nations that are round about you; of *them* shall ye buy male and female domestics." "Moreover, of the children of the foreigners that do sojourn among you, of *them* shall ye buy, and of their families that are with you, which they begat in your land, and *they* shall be your permanent resource." "And ye shall take them as a *perpetual* source of supply to which your children after you shall resort for servants. ALWAYS *of them* shall ye serve yourselves." The design of the passage is manifest from its structure. So far from being a permission to purchase slaves, it was a prohibition to employ Israelites for a certain term and in a certain grade of service, and to point out the *class* of persons from which they were to get their supply of servants, and the *way* in which they were to get them.*

OBJECTION IV. "*If thy brother that dwelleth by thee be waxen poor, and be sold unto thee, thou shalt*

---

* Rabbi Leeser, who translated from the German the work entitled "Instruction in the Mosaic Religion," by Prof. Jholson, of the Jewish seminary at Frankfort-on-the-Main, in his comment on these verses, says, "It must be observed that it was prohibited to SUBJECT *a stranger to slavery.* The *buying* of slaves *alone* is permitted, but not stealing them."

*not compel him to serve as a* BONDSERVANT, *but as
an* HIRED-SERVANT, *and as a sojourner shall he be
with thee, and shall serve thee unto the year of
jubilee.*" Lev. xxv. 39, 40.

As only *one* class is called "*hired,*" it is inferred
that servants of the other class were *not paid* for
their labor; and that God, while thundering anathemas
against those who "used their neighbor's service without wages, granted a special indulgence to his chosen
people to force others to work, and rob them of their
earnings. The inference that "*hired*" is synonymous
with *paid,* and that those servants not *called* "hired"
were *not paid* for their labor, is a mere assumption.
The meaning of the verb to *hire* is to procure *temporary* service for wages. That is also the meaning of
the Hebrew word "*saukar.*" It is not used when the
procurement of *permanent* service is spoken of. The
every-day distinctions in this matter are well known.
In many families, the domestics perform only the
*regular* work. Whatever is occasional merely, as the
washing of a family, is done by persons hired expressly
for that purpose. The familiar distinction between
the two classes, is "servants" and "hired help." *Both*
classes are *paid.* One is permanent, and the other occasional and temporary, and *therefore* called "hired."*
A variety of particulars are recorded distinguishing

---

* To suppose a servant robbed of his earnings because he
is not called a *hired* servant, is profound induction! If I
employ a man at twelve dollars a month to work my farm,
he is my "*hired*" man; but if *I give him such a portion of the
crop,* or, in other words, if he works my farm "*on shares,*" he
is no longer called a "*hired*" man. Yet he works the same

*hired* from *bought* servants. 1. Hired servants were paid daily at the close of their work. Lev. xix. 13; Deut. xxiv. 14, 15; Job vii. 2; Matt. xx. 8. *"Bought"* servants were paid in advance (a reason for their being called *bought*), and those that went out at the seventh year received a *gratuity*. Deut. xv. 12, 13. 2. The "hired" were paid *in money*, the "bought" received their *gratuity*, at least, in grain, cattle, and the product of the vintage. Deut. xv. 14. 3. The "hired" *lived* in their own families, the "bought" were a part of their masters' families. 4. The "hired" supported their families out of their wages; the "bought" and their families were supported by the master *besides* their wages. 5. Hired servants were expected to have more *working hours* in the day than the bought servants. This we infer from the fact, that "a hireling's day" was a sort of proverbial phrase, meaning a *full* day—no subtraction of time being made from it. So, *a hireling's year* signifies an entire year without abatement. Job vii. 1; xiv. 6; Isa. xvi. 14; xxi. 16.

The "bought" servants were, *as a class, superior to the hired*—were more trustworthy, more prized, had

farm, in the same way, with the same teams and tools; and does the same amount of work in the year, and perhaps clears twenty dollars a month, instead of twelve. As he is no longer called "hired," and still works my farm, my neighbors sagely infer, that I *rob* him of his earnings, and with all the gravity of owls, pronounce their oracular decision, and hoot it abroad. My neighbors are deep divers! like some theological professors, they not only go to the bottom, but come up covered with the tokens.

greater privileges, and a more elevated station in society.   1. They were intimately incorporated with the family of the master, were guests at family festivals and social solemnities, from which hired servants were excluded.   Lev. xxii. 10, 11; Ex. xii. 43, 45. 2. Their interests were far more identified with those of their masters' family.   They were often, actually or prospectively, heirs of their masters' estates, as in the case of Eliezer, of Ziba, and the sons of Bilhah and Zilpah.   When there were no sons, or when they were unworthy, bought servants were made heirs. Prov. xvii. 2.   We find traces of this usage in the New Testament.   "But when the husbandmen saw him, they reasoned among themselves, saying, This is the *heir;* come, let us kill him, *that the inheritance may be ours.*"  Luke xx. 14.   In no instance does a *hired* servant inherit his master's estate.    3. Marriages took place between servants and their masters' daughters.   "Sheshan had a *servant,* an Egyptian, whose name was Jarha.   And Sheshan gave his daughter to Jarha, his servant, to wife."  1 Chron. ii. 34, 35.   There is no instance of a *hired* servant forming such an alliance.    4. Bought servants and their descendants were treated with marked affection and respect as members of the family.*   The treatment of

---

* "For the *purchased servant* who is an Israelite, or proselyte, shall fare as his master.   The master shall not eat fine bread, and his servant bread of bran.   Nor yet drink old wine, and give his servant new; nor sleep on soft pillows, and bedding, and his servant on straw.   I say unto you, that·he that gets a *purchased* servant does well to make him as his friend, or he will prove to his employer as if he got

Abraham's servants. Gen. xxiv. and xviii. 1–7; the
intercourse between Gideon and Phurah, Judg. vii.
10, 11; Saul and his servant, 1 Sam. ix. 5, 22;
Jonathan and his servant, 1 Sam. xiv. 1–14, and
Elisha and Gehazi are illustrations. The tenderness
exercised towards home-born servants or the children
of *handmaids*, and the strength of the tie that bound
them to the family, are employed by the Psalmist to
illustrate the regard of God for him and his own
endearing relation to him, when in the last extremity
he prays, "Save the son of thy *handmaid.*" Ps.
lxxxvi. 16. So also in Ps. cxvi. 16. "Oh Lord,
truly I am thy servant; I am thy servant, and the son
of thy *handmaid.*" Also Jer. ii. 14: "Is Israel a
servant? Is he a *home-born*?* WHY IS HE
SPOILED?" No such tie seems to have existed between *hired* servants and their masters. Their
untrustworthiness was proverbial. John x. 12, 13.
They were reckoned at but half the value of bought
servants. Deut. xv. 18. None but the *lowest class*
of the people engaged as hired servants, and the
kinds of labor assigned to them required little knowledge and skill. No persons seem to have become
hired servants, except such as were forced to it from
extreme poverty. The hired servant is called "poor
and needy," and the reason assigned by God why he
should be paid as soon as he had finished his work is,

himself a master."—*Maimonides, in Mishna Kiddushim.* Chap.
1, Sec. 2.

* Our translators, in rendering it "Is he a home-born
SLAVE," were wise beyond what was written.

"For *he is poor*, and setteth his heart upon it."
Deut. xxiv. 14, 15. See also, 1 Sam. ii. 5. Various
passages show the low repute and inferior character
of the class from which they were hired. Judg. ix.
4; 1 Sam. ii. 5. The superior condition of bought
servants is manifest in the high trusts confided to
them, and in their dignity and authority in the household. In no instance is a *hired* servant thus dis-
tinguished. The *bought* servant is manifestly the
master's representative in the family, sometimes with
plenipotentiary powers over adult children, even
negotiating marriage for them. Abraham abjured
his servant not to take a wife for Isaac of the
daughters of the Canaanites. The servant himself
selected her. Servants had discretionary power in
the management of their masters' estates : "And the
servant took ten camels of the camels of his master,
*for all the goods of his master were in his hand.*"
Gen. xxiv. 10. The reason assigned is not that such
was Abraham's direction, but that the servant had
discretionary control. They had the same power in
the *disposal of property.* Gen. xxiv. 22, 30, 53.
The condition of Ziba, in the house of Mephibosheth
is a case in point. So is Prov. xvii. 2. Distinct
traces of this estimation are to be found in the New
Testament, Matt. xxiv. 45 ; Luke xii. 42, 44. In the
parable of the talents, the master seems to have set
up each of his servants in trade with a large capital.
The unjust steward had large *discretionary* power,
was "accused of wasting his master's goods," and
manifestly regulated with his debtors the *terms* of

settlement. Luke xvi. 4–8. Such trusts were never reposed in *hired* servants.

The inferior condition of *hired* servants is illustrated in the parable of the prodigal son. When he came to himself, the memory of his home, and of the abundance enjoyed by even the *lowest* class of servants in his father's household, while he was perishing with hunger among the swine and husks, so filled him with anguish that he exclaimed, "How many *hired* servants of my father have bread enough and to spare, and I perish with hunger!" His proud heart broke. "I will arise," he cried, "and go to my father;" and then to assure his father of the depth of his humility, resolved to add, "Make me as one of thy *hired* servants." If *hired* servants were the *superior* class —to bespeak the situation savored little of that sense of unworthiness that seeks the dust with hidden face, and cries "unclean!" Unhumbled nature *climbs;* or if it falls, clings fast where first it may. Humility sinks of its own weight, and in the lowest deep digs lower. The design of the parable was to illustrate, on the one hand, the joy of God as he beholds afar off the returning sinner, "seeking an injured father's face," who runs to clasp and bless him with an unchiding welcome; and on the other, the contrition of the penitent, turning homeward with tears from his wanderings, his stricken spirit breaking with its ill-desert he sobs aloud, "The lowest place! I can abide no other!" Or in those inimitable words, "Father, I have sinned against heaven, and in thy sight, and am no more worthy to be called thy son; make me as one of thy HIRED servants." The supposition that *hired* servants were the *highest* class takes from the parable an element of winning beauty and pathos.

It is manifest that *one* class of servants was on terms of equality with the children and other members of the family. Hence the force of Paul's declaration, Gal. iv. 1, "Now I say unto you that the heir, so long as he is a child, DIFFERETH NOTHING FROM A SERVANT, though he be lord of all." If this were the *hired* class, the prodigal was a sorry specimen of humility. Would our Lord have put such language upon the lips of one held up by himself as a model of humility, to illustrate its deep sense of all ill-desert? If this be *humility*, put it on stilts, and set it a strutting, while pride takes lessons, and blunders in aping it.

Israelites and strangers belong indiscriminately to *each* class of the servants, the *bought* and the *hired*. That those in the former class rose in the family to honors and authority, which were not conferred on *hired* servants, has been shown. It should be added, however, that in the enjoyment of privileges merely *political*, the hired servants from the *Israelites* were more favored than the bought servants from the *strangers*. No one from the strangers was eligible to the highest office, nor could he own the soil. This last disability seems to have been one reason for the different periods of service required of the two classes of bought servants. The Israelite was to serve six years—the stranger until the jubilee. As the strangers could not own the soil, nor houses, except within walled towns, they would naturally attach themselves to Israelitish families. Those who were

11

wealthy, or skilled in manufactures, instead of becoming servants would have servants for their own use; and as inducements for the strangers to become servants to the Israelites were greater than persons of their own nation could hold out to them, these wealthy strangers would naturally procure the poorer Israelites for servants. Lev. xxv. 47. In a word, such was the political condition of the strangers, that the Jewish polity offered a virtual bounty to such as would become permanent servants, and thus secure those privileges already enumerated, and for their children in the second generation a permanent inheritance. Ezek. xlvii. 21–23. None but the wealthy would be likely to decline such offers. On the other hand, the Israelites, owning all the soil, and an inheritance of land being a sacred possession, to hold it free of incumbrance was with every Israelite a point both of family honor and personal character. 1 Kings xxi. 3. Hence, to forego the control of one's inheritance, after the division of the paternal domain, or to be kept out of it after having acceded to it, was a burden grievous to be borne. To mitigate as much as possible such a calamity, the law released the Israelitish servant at the end of six* years; as, during that time

---

* Another reason for protracting the service until the seventh year seems to have been the coincidence of that period with other arrangements in the Jewish economy. Its pecuniary responsibilities, social relations, and general internal structure, were *graduated* upon a septennial scale. Besides, as those Israelites who had become servants through poverty, would not sell themselves, till other expedients to recruit their finances had failed—(Lev. xxv. 35)—their

—if of the first class—the partition of the patrimonial
land might have taken place ; or, if of the second,
enough money might have been earned to disencumber
his estate, and thus he might assume his station as a
lord of the soil.   If neither contingency had occurred,
then after another six years the opportunity was again
offered, and so on, until the jubilee.   So, while strong
motives urged the Israelite to discontinue his service
as soon as the exigency had passed which made him
a servant, every consideration impelled the *stranger*
to *prolong* his term of service ;* and the same kindness
which dictated the law of six years' service for the
Israelite assigned as the general rule, a much longer
period to the Gentile servant, who had every inducement to protract the term.   It should be borne in
mind that adult Jews ordinarily became servants,
only as a temporary expedient to relieve themselves
from embarrassment, and ceased to be such when that
object was effected.   The poverty that forced them
to it was a calamity, and their service was either a
means of relief or a measure of prevention ; not pursued as a permanent business, but resorted to on
emergencies—a sort of episode in the main scope of
their lives ; whereas with the strangers it was a *permanent employment*, pursued both as a *means* of
bettering their own condition, and that of their pos-

*becoming servants* proclaimed such a state of their affairs as
demanded the labor of a *course of years* fully to reinstate
them.

* The stranger had the same inducements to prefer a long
term of service that those who cannot own land have to prefer a long *lease*.

terity, and as an *end* for its own sake, conferring on them privileges, and a social estimation not otherwise attainable.

We see from the foregoing why servants purchased from the heathen are called, by way of distinction, *the* servants (not *bondmen*). 1. They followed it as a *permanent business.* 2. Their term of service was *much longer* than that of the other class. 3. As a class, they greatly outnumbered the Israelitish servants. 4. All the strangers that dwelt in the land were *tributaries*, required to pay an annual tax to the government, either in money, or in public service (called a "*tribute of bond-service*"); in other words, all the strangers were *national servants* to the Israelites, and the same Hebrew word used to designate *individual* servants, equally designates *national* servants. 2 Sam. viii. 2, 6, 14; 2 Chron. viii. 7–9; Deut. xx. 11; 2 Sam. x. 19; 1 Kings ix. 21, 22; 1 Kings iv. 21; Gen. xxvii. 29. The same word is applied to the Israelites, when they paid tribute to other nations. 2 Kings xvii. 3; Judg. iii. 8, 14; Gen. xlix. 15. Another distinction between the Jewish and Gentile bought servants was in their *kinds* of service. The servants from the strangers were properly the *domestics*, or household servants, employed in all family work, in offices of personal attendance, and in such mechanical labor as was required by increasing wants and needed repairs. The Jewish bought servants seem almost exclusively *agricultural.* Besides being better fitted for it by previous habits, agriculture, and the tending of cattle, were regarded by the Israelites as the most honorable of all occupations. After Saul was elected king, and escorted to Gibeah, the next report of him is, "*And behold Saul came after the herd out of the field.*" 1 Sam. xi. 5. Elisha "was ploughing with twelve yoke of oxen." 1 Kings xix. 19. King Uzziah "loved husbandry." 2 Chron. xxvi. 10. Gideon *was* "*threshing wheat*" when called to lead the host against the Midianites. Judg. vi. 11. The superior honorableness of agriculture is shown in that it was protected and supported by the fundamental law of the theocracy—God thus indicating it as the chief prop of the government. The Israelites were permanent fixtures on their soil. To be agriculturists on their own patrimonial inheritances was the grand claim to honorable estimation. When Ahab proposed to Naboth to buy his vineyard, king though he was, he might well have anticipated from an Israelitish freeholder, just such an indignant outburst as that which his proposal drew forth! "And Naboth said to Ahab, The Lord forbid it me that I should give the inheritance of my fathers unto thee!" 1 Kings xxi. 2, 3. Agriculture being pre-eminently a *Jewish* employment, to assign an Israelite to other employments as a business was to break up his habits, do violence to cherished predilections, and put him to a kind of labor in which he had no skill, and which he deemed degrading.* In short, it was, in the earlier

---

* The Babylonish captivity seems to have greatly modified Jewish usage in this respect. Before that event, their cities were comparatively small, and few were engaged in mechanical or mercantile employments. Afterward their cities enlarged apace and trades multiplied.

ages of the Mosaic system, practically to *unjew* him,
—a rigor grievous to be borne, as it annihilated a
visible distinction between the descendants of Abraham and strangers. *To guard this and another
fundamental distinction,* God instituted the regulation, "If thy brother that dwelleth by thee be waxen
poor, and be sold unto thee, thou shalt not compel
him to serve as a bond-servant." In other words,
thou shalt not put him to servant's work—to the
business and into the condition of domestics. In the
Persian version it is translated, "Thou shalt not
assign to him the work of *servitude.*" In the Septuagint, "He shall not serve thee with the service of a
*domestic.*" In the Syriac, "Thou shalt not employ
him after the manner of servants." In the Samaritan,
"Thou shalt not require him to serve in the service
of a servant." In the Targum of Onkelos, "He shall
not serve thee with the service of a household servant."
In the Targum of Jonathan, "Thou shalt not cause
him to serve according to the usages of the servitude
of servants."* The meaning of the passage is, *thou
shalt not assign him to the same grade, nor put him
to the same service, as that of permanent domestics.*

---

* Jarchi's comment on "Thou shalt not compel him to
serve as a bond-servant" is, "The Hebrew servant is not to
be required to do anything which is accounted degrading—
such as all offices of personal attendance, as loosing his
master's shoe-latchet, bringing him water to wash his hands
and feet, waiting on him at table, dressing him, carrying
things to and from the bath. The Hebrew servant is to work
with his master as a son or brother, in the business of his
farm, or other labor, until his legal release."

The remainder of the regulation is, *"But as an hired servant, and as a sojourner, shall he be with thee."* Hired servants were not incorporated into the families of their masters ; they retained their family organization, without the surrender of any domestic privilege, honor, or authority ; and this, even though they resided under the same roof with their master. The same substantially may be said of the sojourner, though he was not the owner of the land which he cultivated, and, of course, had not the control of an inheritance ; yet he was not in a condition that implied subjection, or that demanded the surrender of any *right*, or exacted from him any homage, or stamped him with any inferiority ; unless it be supposed that a degree of inferiority would naturally attach to a state of *dependence*, however qualified. While bought servants were associated with their master's families at meals, at the Passover, and at other family festivals, hired servants and sojourners were not. Ex. xii. 44, 45 ; Lev. xxii. 10, 11. They were not subject to the authority of their masters in any such sense as the master's wife, children, and bought-servants. Hence the only form of oppressing hired servants spoken of in the Scriptures as practicable to masters, is that *of keeping back their wages.* To have taken away such privileges in the case under consideration would have been pre-eminent *"rigor ;"* for it was not a servant born in the house of a master, nor a minor, whose minority had been sold by the father, neither was it one who had not yet acceded to his inheritance ; nor, finally, one who had received the *assignment* of his inheritance, but was working off from it an incumbrance, before entering upon its possession and control. But it was that of *the head of a family* who had known better days, forced to relinquish the loved inheritance of his fathers, with the competence and respectful consideration its possession secured to him, and to be indebted to a neighbor for sustenance and employment. Still one consolation cheers him in the house of his pilgrimage—he is an *Israelite—Abraham is his father;* and now in his calamity he clings closer than ever to the distinction conferred by his birth-right. To rob him of this were "the unkindest cut of all." To have assigned him to a grade of service filled only by those whose permanent business was serving, would have been to "rule over him with" peculiar "rigor." "Thou shalt not compel him to serve as a bond-servant," or, literally, *thou shalt not serve thyself with him, with the service of a servant,* guaranties his political privileges, and a kind and grade of service comporting with his character and relations as an Israelite. And "as a *hired* servant, and as a sojourner, shall he be with thee," secures to him his family organization, the respect due to its head, and the general consideration resulting from such a station. Being already in possession of his inheritance, and the head of a household, the law so arranged the conditions of his service as to *alleviate* the calamity which had reduced him from independence and authority to penury and subjection. The import of the command which concludes this topic in the forty-third verse ("Thou shalt not rule over him with rigor") is manifestly this : Thou shalt not disregard those differences in previous associations, station, authority, and political privileges, upon which this regulation is based; for to hold this class of servants *irrespective* of these distinctions, and annihilating them, is to "rule with rigor." The same command is repeated in the forty-sixth verse, and applied to the distinction between servants of Jewish and those of Gentile extraction, and forbids the overlooking of distinctive Jewish peculiarities, the disregard of which would be *rigorous* in the extreme.* The construction commonly put upon the phrase, "rule with rigor," and the inference drawn from it, have an air vastly oracular. It is interpreted to mean, "you shall not make him a chattel, and strip him of legal protection, nor force him to work without wages." The inference is like unto it, viz., since the command forbade such outrages upon the Israelites, it permitted and commissioned their infliction upon the strangers! Such a construction captivates scoffers and libertines; its blasphemy, and loose-reined license, work like a charm upon them. What boots it to reason against such rampant affinities! In Ex. i. 13, it is said that the Egyptians "made the children of Israel to *serve* with rigor." This rigor is affirmed of the *amount of labor* extorted, and the *mode* of the exaction. The expression, "serve with rigor," is never applied to the

* The disabilities of the strangers, which were distinctions, based on a different national descent, and important to the preservation of national characteristics and a national worship, did not affect their *social* estimation. They were regarded according to their character and worth as *persons*, irrespective of their foreign origin, employment, and political condition.

service of servants under the Mosaic system. The
phrase, "Thou shalt not RULE over him with rigor,"
does not prohibit unreasonable exactions of labor, nor
inflictions of cruelty. Such were provided against
otherwise. But it forbids confounding the distinctions
between a Jew and a stranger, by assigning the former
to the same grade of service, for the same term of time,
and under the same political disabilities as the latter.

We are now prepared to review the condition of
the different classes of servants, with the modifications
peculiar to each class.

In all fundamental rights, all classes of servants were
on an absolute equality ; all were equally protected
by law in their persons, character, property, and social
relations ; all were voluntary, all were compensated
for their labor, and released from it nearly one-half of
the days in each year ; all were furnished with stated
instruction ; none in either class were in any sense
articles of property ; all were regarded as *men*, with
the rights, interests, hopes, and destinies of *men*. In
all these respects, *all* classes of servants among the
Israelites formed but ONE CLASS. The *different*
classes, and the differences in *each* class, were, 1.
*Hired servants*. This class consisted both of Israelites and strangers. Their employments were different.
The *Israelite* was an agricultural servant. The
stranger was a *domestic* and *personal* servant, and in
some instances *mechanical ;* both were occasional and
temporary. Both lived in their own families, their
wages were *money*, and they were paid when their
work was done. 2. *Bought servants* (including those
"born in the house"). This class, also, consisted of

Israelites and strangers, with the same difference in their kinds of employment. Both were paid in advance,* and neither was temporary. The Israelitish servant, with the exception of the *freeholder*, completed his term in six years. The stranger was a permanent servant, continuing until the jubilee. A marked distinction obtained also between different classes of *Jewish* bought servants. Ordinarily, they were merged in their master's family, and, like his wife and children, subject to his authority; and, like them, protected by law from its abuse. But the *freeholder* was an exception; his family relations and authority remained unaffected, nor was he subjected as an inferior to the control of his master, though dependent on him for employment.

It should be kept in mind that *both* classes of servants, Israelites and strangers, not only enjoyed *equal, natural, and religious rights*, but *all the*

---

* The payment- *in advance* doubtless lessened the price; the servant thus having the use of the money, and the master assuming all the risks of life and health for labor; at the expiration of the six years' contract, the master was obliged by law to release the servant with a liberal gratuity. The reason assigned for this is, "he hath been worth a double hired servant unto thee in serving thee six years;"—as if it had been said, as you have experienced no loss from the risks of life, and ability to labor, incurred in the purchase, and which lessened the price, and as, by being your servant for six years, he has saved you the time and trouble of looking up and hiring laborers on emergencies, therefore, "thou shalt furnish him liberally," &c.

This gratuity at the close of the service shows the *principle* of the relation; *equivalent* for value received.

*civil and political privileges* enjoyed by those of
their own people who were *not* servants.  They also
shared in common with them the political disabilities
which appertained to all strangers, whether servants
of Jewish masters, or masters of Jewish servants.
Further, the disabilities of the servants from the
strangers were exclusively *political* and *national*.
1. They could not own the soil.  2. They were
ineligible to office.  3. They were assigned to
employments less honorable ; agriculture being regarded as fundamental to the existence of the state,
other employments were in less repute, and deemed
*unjewish.*

Finally, the strangers, whether servants or masters,
were all protected equally with the descendants of
Abraham.  In respect to political privileges, their
condition was much like that of unnaturalized foreigners in the United States ; who, whatever their
wealth or intelligence, or moral principle, or love for
our institutions, can neither vote, nor own the soil, nor
be eligible to office.  Let a native American be thus
suddenly loaded with the disabilities of an alien, and
what to the foreigner would be a light matter, to *him*
would be the severity of *rigor.*  The recent condition
of the Jews and Catholics in England is another
illustration.  Rothschild, the late London banker,
though the richest private citizen in the world, and
perhaps master of a score of English servants, was,
as a subject of the government, inferior to the lowest
among them.  Suppose an English millionaire were
by law deprived of power to own the soil, of eligibility
to office, and of the electoral franchise, would he think

it a misapplication of language, if it were said, the
government "rules over him with rigor?" And yet
his person, property, reputation, conscience, all his
social relations, the disposal of his time, the right of
locomotion at pleasure, and of natural liberty in all
respects, are as much protected by law as the Lord
Chancellor's.

FINALLY. As the Mosaic system was a great compound type, rife with meaning in doctrine and duty,
the practical power of the whole depended upon the
exact observance of those distinctions and relations
which constituted its significancy. Hence, the care
to preserve inviolate the distinction between a
*descendant of Abraham* and a *stranger*, even when
the stranger was a proselyte, had gone through the
initiatory ordinances, entered the congregation, and
become incorporated with the Israelites by family
alliance. The regulation laid down in Ex. xxi. 2–6,
is an illustration. In this case, the Israelitish servant, whose term expired in six years, had married
one of his master's *permanent female domestics;* but
her marriage did not release her master from *his* part
of the contract for her whole term of service, nor from
his legal obligation to support and educate her children. Neither did it do away that distinction which
marked her national descent by a specific *grade* and
*term* of service, nor impair her obligation to fulfil *her*
part of the contract. Her relations as a permanent
domestic grew out of a distinction guarded with great
care throughout the Mosaic system. To render it
void would have been to divide the system against
itself. This God would not tolerate. Nor, on the

12

other hand, would he permit the master to throw off
the responsibility of instructing her children, nor the
care and expense of their infancy and rearing. He
was bound to support and educate them, and all her
children born during her term of service. The whole
arrangement illustrates that tender regard for the
interests of all, which marks the Mosaic system.* By
this law, the children had secured to them a mother's
care. If the husband loved his family he could compel
his master to keep him, whether he had occasion for
his services or not. If he did not love them, to be rid
of him was a blessing; and in that case, the regulation
would prove an act for the relief of an afflicted family.
The release of the servant in the seventh year neither
absolved him from the obligations of marriage, nor
shut him out from the society of his family. He could
probably procure a service at no great distance from
them, and might often do it, to get higher wages, or a
kind of employment better suited to his taste and skill.
The great number of days on which the law released
servants from regular labor would enable him to spend
much more time with his family than can be spent by
most of the agents of our benevolent societies with
*their* families, or by many merchants, editors, artists,
&c., whose daily business is in a city, while their
families reside from five to fifty miles in the country.

* Whoever studies the Mosaic Institutes with a teachable
spirit will feel the power of that solemn interrogatory of God
to Israel, when he had set before them all his statutes and
ordinances: "What nation is there so great, that hath
statutes and judgments *so* RIGHTEOUS as *all* this law which I
set before you this day?" Deut. iv. 8.

We conclude this inquiry by considering one more objection. "The enslavement of the Canaanites by the Israelites was appointed by God as a commutation of the punishment of death denounced against them for their sins."* Only *one* statute was ever given respecting the disposition to be made of the inhabitants of Canaan. If the sentence of death was pronounced against them, and afterwards *commuted*, when? where? by whom? and in what terms was the commutation, and where is it recorded? Grant that all the Canaanites were sentenced to unconditional extermination; how can a right to *enslave* them be drawn from such premises? The punishment of death is one of the highest recognitions of man's moral nature. It proclaims him rational, accountable, deserving death for having done his utmost to cheapen human life, when the proof of its priceless worth lived in his own nature. But to make man a *slave* cheapens to nothing *universal human nature*, and, instead of healing a wound, gives a death-stab. What! repair an injury to rational being in the robbery of one of its rights, by not only robbing it of all, but by annihilating their *foundation*, the distinction between persons and things? To make a man a chattel is not the *punishment*, but in principle the

* In the prophecy, Gen. ix. 25, the subjection of the Canaanites as a conquered people rendering tribute to other nations is foretold. The fulfilment of this prediction seems to have commenced in the subjection of the Canaanites to the Israelites as tributaries. If the Israelites had exterminated them, as the objector asserts they were commanded to do, the prediction would have been *falsified*.

*annihilation* of a *human* being, and, so far as it goes,
of *all* human beings. Here a question arises of
sufficient importance for a separate dissertation ; but
it must, for the present, be disposed of in a few para-
graphs. WERE THE CANAANITES SENTENCED BY GOD
TO INDIVIDUAL AND UNCONDITIONAL EXTERMINATION ?
The directions as to the disposal of the Canaanites
are mainly in the following passages : Ex. xxiii. 23–
33 ; xxxiv. 11 ; Deut. vii. 16–24 ; ix. 3 ; xxxi. 3–5.
In these verses, the Israelites are commanded to
" destroy the Canaanites," to " drive out," "consume,"
"utterly overthrow," "put out," "dispossess them,"
&c. Did these commands enjoin the universal
destruction of the *individuals*, or merely of the *body
politic ?* The word *hārām*, to destroy, signifies
*national* as well as individual destruction ; the
destruction of *political* existence equally with *personal ;* of governmental organization equally with the
lives of the subjects. Besides, if we interpret the
words destroy, consume, overthrow, &c., to mean *personal* destruction, what meaning shall we give to the
expressions, " drive out before thee," " cast out before
thee," " expel," " put out," " dispossess," &c., which
are used in the same and in parallel passages ? In
addition to those quoted above, see Josh. iii. 10 ; xvii.
18 ; xxii. 5 ; xxiv. 18 ; Judg. i. 20, 29–35 ; vi. 9. " I
will *destroy* all the people to whom thou shalt come,
and I will make all thine enemies *turn their backs
unto thee.*" Ex. xxiii. 27. Here " *all their
enemies*" were to *turn their backs*, and " *all the
people*" to be " *destroyed.*" Does this mean that God
would let all their *enemies* escape, but kill their

*friends*, or that he would *first* kill " all the people,"
and THEN make them " turn their backs," an army of
runaway corpses ?　In Josh. xxiv. 8, God says, speaking of the Amorites, " I *destroyed* them from before
you."　In the 18th verse of the same chapter, it is
said, " The Lord *drave out* from before us all the
people, even the Amorites which dwelt in the land."
In Num. xxxii. 39, we are told that " the children of
Machir, the son of Manasseh, went to Gilead, and
took it, and *dispossessed* the Amorite which was in
it."　If these commands required the destruction of
all the *individuals*, the Mosaic law was at war with
itself; for directions as to the treatment of native residents form a large part of it.　See Lev. xix. 34 ; xxv.
35, 36 ; xxiv. 22 ; Ex. xxiii. 9 ; xxii. 21 ; Deut. i. 16,
17 ; x. 17, 19 ; xxvii. 19.　We find, also, that provision was made for them in the cities of refuge.　Num.
xxxv. 15 ;—the gleanings of the harvest and vintage
were theirs.　Lev. xix. 9, 10 ; xxiii. 22 ;—the blessings of the Sabbath, Ex. xx. 10 ;—the privilege of
offering sacrifices secured, Lev. xxii. 18 ; and stated
religious instruction provided for them, Deut. xxxi. 9,
12.　Now, does this same law require the *individual*
*extermination* of those whose lives and interests it
thus protects ?　These laws were given to the Israelites long *before* they entered Canaan ; and they must
have inferred from them that a multitude of the inhabitants of the land were to *continue in it*, under their
government.　Again, Joshua was selected as the
leader of Israel to execute God's threatenings upon
Canaan.　He had no discretionary power.　God's
commands were his official instructions.　Going be-

yond them would have been usurpation; refusing to
carry them out, rebellion and treason.    Saul was
rejected from being king for disobeying God's commands in a single instance.    If God commanded the
individual destruction of all the Canaanites, Joshua
disobeyed him in every instance.    For at his death
the Israelites still "*dwelt among them*," and each
nation is mentioned by name.    Judg. i. 27–36; and
yet we are told that Joshua " left nothing undone of
all that the Lord commanded Moses ;" and that he
"took all that land."    Josh. xi. 15–22.    Also, that
" there *stood not a man* of *all* their enemies before
them."    Josh. xxi. 44.    How can this be if the command to "destroy," "destroy utterly," &c., enjoined
*individual* extermination, and the command to drive
out, unconditional expulsion from the country rather
than their expulsion from the *possession* or *ownership* of it, as the lords of the soil?    That the latter
is the true sense to be attached to those terms we
argue further, from the fact that the same terms
are employed by God to describe the punishment
which he would inflict upon the Israelites, if they
served other gods.    "Ye shall utterly perish," "be
utterly destroyed," "consumed," &c., are some of
them.    See Deut. iv. 26; viii. 19, 20;* Josh. xxiii.

---

* These two verses are so explicit, we quote them entire:
"And it shall be if thou do at all forget the Lord thy God,
and walk after other gods, and serve them, and worship them,
I testify against you this day that ye shall surely *perish:* as
the nations which the Lord destroyed before your face, *so*
shall ye perish."    The following passages are, if possible,
still more explicit: "The Lord shall send upon thee cursing,

12, 13–16; 1 Sam. xii. 25. The Israelites *did* serve other gods, and Jehovah *did* execute upon them his threatenings; and thus himself *interpreted* these threatenings. He subverted their *government*, dispossessed them of their land, divested them of national power, and made them *tributaries*, but did not *exterminate* them. He "destroyed them utterly" as an independent body politic, but not as individuals." Multitudes of the Canaanites were slain, but not a case can be found in which one was either killed or expelled who *acquiesced* in the transfer of the territory and its sovereignty from the inhabitants of the land to the Israelites. Witness the case of Rahab

---

vexation, and rebuke in all that thou settest thine hand unto for to do, until thou be *destroyed*, and until thou perish quickly." "The Lord shall make the pestilence cleave unto thee until he have *consumed* thee." "They (the 'sword,' 'blasting,' &c.) shall pursue thee until thou *perish*." "From heaven shall it come down upon thee till thou be *destroyed*." "All these curses shall come upon thee till thou be *destroyed*." "He shall put a yoke of iron upon thy neck until he have *destroyed* thee." "The Lord shall bring a nation against thee, which shall not regard the person of the old, nor show favor to the young, * * until he have *destroyed* thee." All these, with other similar threatenings of *destruction*, are contained in the twenty-eighth chapter of Deut. See verses 20–25, 45, 48, 51. In the *same* chapter, God declares that, as a punishment for the same transgressions, the Israelites shall "be *removed*" into all the kingdoms of the earth,"—thus showing that the terms employed in the other verses, "destroy," "perish," "perish quickly," "consume," &c., instead of signifying utter, personal destruction, doubtless meant their destruction as an independent nation. In Josh. xxiv. 8, 18, "destroyed" and "drave out," are used synonymously.

and her kindred, and that of the Gibeonites.* The Canaanites knew of the miracles wrought for the Israelites; and that their land had been transferred to them as a judgment for their sins. Josh. ii. 9–11; ix. 9, 10, 24. Many of them were awed by these wonders, and made no resistance. Others came out to battle. These last occupied the fortified cities, were the most inveterate heathen—the aristocracy of idolatry, the kings, the nobility and gentry, the priests, with their crowds of retainers that aided in idolatrous rites, and the military forces, with the chief

* Perhaps it will be objected, that the preservation of the Gibeonites, and of Rahab and her kindred, was a violation of the command of God. We answer, if it had been, we might expect some such intimation. If God had straitly commanded them to *exterminate all the Canaanites*, their pledge to save them alive was neither a repeal of the statute, nor absolution for the breach of it. If *unconditional destruction* was the import of the command, would God have permitted such an act to pass without rebuke? Would he have established such a precedent when Israel had hardly passed the threshold of Canaan, and was then striking the first blow of a half century war? What if they *had* passed their word to Rahab and the Gibeonites? Was that more binding than God's command? So Saul seems to have passed *his* word to Agag; yet Samuel hewed him in pieces, because in saving his life Saul had violated God's command. When Saul sought to slay the Gibeonites in "his zeal for the children of Israel and Judah," God sent upon Israel a three years' famine for it. When David inquired of them what atonement he should make, they say, "The man that devised against us, that we should be destroyed from *remaining in any of the coasts of Israel*, let seven of his sons be delivered," &c. 2 Sam. xxi. 1–6.

profligates of both sexes.    Many facts corroborate the
general position.    Witness that command (Deut.
xxiii. 15, 16), which not only prohibited the surrender
of the fugitive servant to his master, but required the
Israelites to receive him with kindness, permit him to
dwell where he pleased, and to protect and cherish
him.    Whenever any servant, even a Canaanite, fled
from his master to the Israelites, Jehovah, so far from
commanding them to *kill* him, straitly charged them,
" He shall dwell with thee, even among you, in that
place which *he* shall choose—in one of thy gates where
it liketh *him* best—thou shalt not oppress him."  Deut.
xxiii. 16.    The Canaanitish servant, by thus fleeing
to the Israelites, submitted himself as a dutiful subject
to their national government, and pledged his allegiance.    Suppose *all* the Canaanites had thus submitted
themselves to the Jewish theocracy, and conformed to
the requirements of the Mosaic institutes, would not *all*
have been spared upon the same principle that *one* was ?
Again, look at the multitudes of *tributaries* in the
midst of Israel, and that, too, after they had " waxed
strong," and the uttermost nations quaked at the
terror of their name—the Canaanites, Philistines, and
others, who became proselytes—as the Nethenims,
Uriah the Hittite—Rahab, who married one of the
princes of Judah—Jether, an Ishmaelite, who married
Abigail, the sister of David, and was the father of
Amasa, the captain of the host of Israel.    Comp.
1 Chron. ii. 17, with 2 Sam. xvii. 25.—Ittai—the six
hundred Gittites, David's body guard. 2 Sam. xv. 18,
21.    Obededom the Gittite, adopted into the tribe of
Levi.    Comp. 2 Sam. vi. 10, 11, with 1 Chron. xv

18, and xxvi. 4, 5—Jaziz and Obil.  1 Chron. xxvii.
30, 31.   Jephunneh, the Kenezite, Josh. xiv. 6, and
father of Caleb, a ruler of the tribe of Judah.   Numb.
xiii. 2, 6—the Kenites registered in the genealogies of
the tribe of Judah, Judg. i. 16; 1 Chron. ii. 55, and
the one hundred and fifty thousand Canaanites employed by Solomon in the building of the Temple.*
Besides, the greatest miracle on record was wrought to
save a portion of those very Canaanites, and for the
destruction of those who would exterminate them.
Josh. x. 12–14.   Further—the terms employed in the
directions regulating the disposal of the Canaanites,
such as "drive out," "put out," "expel," "dispossess," &c., seem used interchangeably with "consume," "destroy," "overthrow," &c., and thus indicate
the sense in which the latter words are used.   As an
illustration of the meaning generally attached to these
and  similar terms, we  refer  to the  history  of  the
Amalekites.   "I will utterly put out the remembrance
of Amalek from under heaven."  Ex. xvii. 14.   "Thou
shalt blot out the remembrance of Amalek from under
heaven;  thou shalt not forget it."  Deut. xxv. 19.
"Smite Amalek, and *utterly destroy* all that they
have, and spare them not, but slay both man and
woman, infant and suckling, ox and sheep."  1 Sam.
xv. 2, 3.   "Saul smote the Amalekites, and he took

* If the Canaanites were devoted by God to unconditional
extermination, to have employed them in the erection of the
temple, what was it but the climax of impiety?  As well
might they pollute its altars with swine's flesh, or make their
sons pass through the fire to Moloch.

Agag, the king of the Amalekites, alive, and UTTERLY
DESTROYED ALL THE PEOPLE with the edge of the
sword." Verses 7, 8. In verse 20, Saul says, I
have brought Agag, the king of Amalek, and have
*utterly destroyed* the Amalekites." In 1 Sam. xxx.
1, 2, we find the Amalekites marching an army into
Israel, and sweeping everything before them—and this
in about eighteen years after they had *all* been
"UTTERLY DESTROYED!" In 1 Kings ii. 15-17, is
another illustration. We are informed that Joab
remained in Edom six months with all Israel, "until
he had *cut off every male*" in Edom. In the next
verse we learn that Hadad and "certain Edomites"
were not slain. Deut. xx. 16, 17, will probably be
quoted against the preceding view. We argue that
the command in these verses did not include all the
individuals of the Canaanitish nations, but only the
inhabitants of the *cities* (and even those conditionally),
because, only the inhabitants of *cities* are specified—
"of the *cities* of these people thou shalt save alive
nothing that breatheth." Cities then, as now, were
pest-houses of vice; they reeked with abominations
little practised in the country. On this account, their
influence would be far more perilous to the Israelites
than that of the country. Besides, they were the
centres of idolatry—there were the temples and altars,
and idols, and priests, without number. Even their
buildings, streets, and public walks were so many
visibilities of idolatry. The reason assigned in the
18th verse for exterminating them, strengthens the
idea—"that they teach you not to do after all the
abominations which they have done unto their gods."

This would be a reason for exterminating *all* the
nations and individuals *around* them, as all were
idolaters ; but God commanded them, in certain cases,
to spare the inhabitants.  Contact with *any* of them
would be perilous—with the inhabitants of the *cities*
peculiarly, and of the *Canaanitish* cities pre-eminently
so.  The 10th and 11th verses contain the general rule
prescribing the method in which cities were to be
summoned to surrender.  They were first to receive
the offer of peace—if it were accepted, the inhabitants
became *tributaries*—but if they came out against
Israel in battle, the *men* were to be killed, and the
women and little ones saved alive.  The 15th verse
restricts this lenient treatment to the inhabitants of
the cities *afar off.*  The 16th directs as to the disposal of the inhabitants of the Canaanitish cities.
They were to save alive "nothing that breathed."
The common mistake has been, in supposing that the
command of the 15th verse refers to the *whole system
of directions preceding,* commencing with the 10th,
whereas it manifestly refers only to the *inflictions*
specified in the 12th, 13th, and 14th, making a distinction between those *Canaanitish* cities that *fought,*
and the cities *afar off* that fought—in one case, destroying the males and females, and in the other, the
*males* only.  The offer of peace, and the *conditional
preservation,* were as really guarantied to *Canaanitish*
cities as to others.  Their inhabitants were not to be
exterminated, unless they came out against Israel in
battle.  Whatever be the import of the commands
respecting the Canaanites, the Israelites did *not*
utterly exterminate them.  If entire and unconditional

extermination was the command of God, it was *never*
obeyed by the Israelites; consequently, the truth of
God stood pledged to consign *them* to the same doom
which he had pronounced upon the Canaanites, but
which they had refused to visit upon them. "If ye
will not drive out all the inhabitants of the land from
before you, then it shall come to pass that * * *I shall
do unto you as I thought to do unto them.*" Num.
xxxiii. 55, 56. As the Israelites were not exterminated, we infer that God did not pronounce *that*
doom upon them; and as he *did* pronounce upon them
the *same* doom, whatever it was, which they should
*refuse* to visit upon the Canaanites, it follows that
the doom of unconditional *extermination* was *not* pronounced against the Canaanites. But let us settle this
question by the "law and the testimony." "There
was not a city that made peace with the children of
Israel, save the Hivites, the inhabitants of Gibeon :
all others they took in battle. For it was of the Lord
to harden their hearts, that they should COME OUT
AGAINST ISRAEL IN BATTLE, that he might destroy
them utterly, and that they might have no favor, but
that he might destroy them, as the Lord commanded
Moses." Josh. xi. 19, 20. That is, if they had not
come out against Israel in battle, they would have had
"favor" shown them, and would not have been
"*destroyed utterly.*" The great design was to *transfer the territory* of the Canaanites to the Israelites.
and along with it. *absolute sovereignty in every
respect;* to annihilate their political organizations.
civil polity, and jurisprudence, and their systems of

13

religion, with all its rights and appendages; and to substitute therefor, a pure theocracy, administered by Jehovah, with the Israelites as His representatives and agents. In a word, the people were to be *denationalized*, their political existence annihilated, their idol temples, altars, groves, images, pictures, and heathen rites destroyed, and themselves put under tribute. Those who resisted the execution of Jehovah's purpose were to be killed, while those who submitted to it were to be spared. All had the choice of these alternatives, either free egress out of the land ;* or acquiescence in the decree, with life and residence as tributaries, under the protection of the government; or resistance to the execution of the decree, with death. "*And it shall come to pass, if they will diligently learn the ways of my people, to swear by my name, the Lord liveth, as they taught my people to swear by Baal;* THEN SHALL THEY BE BUILT IN THE MIDST OF MY PEOPLE."

[The original design of the preceding inquiry embraced a much wider range of topics. It was soon found, however, that to fill up the outline would be to

* Suppose all the Canaanitish nations had abandoned their territory to the tidings of Israel's approach, did God's command require the Israelites to chase them to ends of the earth, and hunt them down, until every Canaanite was destroyed? It is too preposterous for belief; and yet it follows legitimately from that construction which interprets the terms "consume," "destroy," "destroy utterly," &c. to mean unconditional, individual extermination.

make a volume. Much of the foregoing has therefore been thrown into a mere series of *indices*, to trains of thought and classes of proof, which, however limited or imperfect, may afford some facilities to those who have little leisure for protracted investigation.]

# APPENDIX.

THE foregoing work, as may be seen, is confined to an examination of the Old Testament. It was the design of the author at one time to include an inquiry into the teachings of the New Testament on the same subject, and the alleged sanction of slavery in the example and teachings of our Lord and his Apostles; but he was deterred from entering upon this, lest what he intended for a tract should swell into a large volume.

As some may, however, think the work incomplete without some notice of the teaching of the New Testament, we have subjoined a few extracts from an excellent address issued by the *Presbyterian Synod of Kentucky*, in 1835.

After pointing out the enormity of the evils of slavery, the *Synod* proceeds to say :—

"We have exhibited fairly, but briefly, the nature and effects of slavery. For the truth of our facts, we refer to your own observations; for the correctness of our reasoning, we appeal to your judgments and consciences. What, then, must we conclude? Is slavery a system which Christians should sanction or even tolerate, if their efforts can avail to abolish it? The reply is often made, ' *God's word sanctions slavery, it cannot therefore be sinful. It cannot be our duty to relinquish our power over our slaves, or the Bible would have enjoined it upon us to do so.'*• We will not attempt to elaborate argument against this plea for slavery—it needs no such answer. A few observations will suffice to show its utter fallacy.

"We are told that the apostles gave to Christian masters and Christian servants directions for the regulation of their mutual conduct. True; and these directions will be valuable while the world lasts—for so long, we doubt not, will *the relation of master and servant exist.* But how do such directions license holding of *slaves?* *The terms which the apostles use in giving these precepts, are the same terms which they would have used had there been no slaves upon the earth.* Many of the masters of that day were indeed slaveholders, and many of the servants were slaves—but should that circumstance have prevented the inspired ambassadors from teaching the duties which devolved upon masters and servants, in every age, and under every form of service? If so, then the fact that rulers at that time were generally tyrants, and the people vassals, should have prevented them from laying down the duties of rulers and people. In the precepts of holy writ, neither *political tyranny* nor *domestic slavery* is countenanced. Nay, if masters complied with the apostolic injunction to them, and gave their servants, as they were directed to do, 'that which is just and equal,' there would be at once an end of all that is properly called slavery.

"The divine right of kings to tyrannize over their subjects, and the unlawfulness of resistance to their authority on the part of the people, were formerly maintained by the very same kind of scriptural arguments which are now advanced in support of slavery. The arguments drawn from the Bible in favor of despotism, are, indeed, much more plausible than those in favor of slavery. We despise the former—how then should we regard the latter?

"It has sometimes been said, that the 'New Testament does not condemn slaveholding in express terms.' And the practice has been advocated, because it has not been denounced. If this assertion were true, and if the Bible only *virtually* denounced it, it would be a sin. No man can righteously continue a practice which God disapproves of, no matter in what form the disapproval is expressed. But the assertion is not true. THE NEW TESTAMENT DOES CONDEMN SLAVEHOLDING, AS PRACTISED AMONG US, IN THE MOST EXPLICIT TERMS FURNISHED BY THE LANGUAGE IN WHICH THE INSPIRED PENMEN WROTE. If a physician, after a minute examination, should tell a patient that his every limb and organ was diseased—if he should enumerate the various parts of his bodily system, the arms, the legs, the head, the stomach, the bowels, &c., and should say of each one of these parts distinctly that it was unsound; could the man depart and say, 'After all, I am not diseased, for the physician has not said, in *express terms*, that my *body* is unsound?' Has he not received a more clear and express declaration of his entirely diseased condition, than if he had been told, in merely general terms, that his *body* was unsound? Thus has God condemned slavery. He has specified the parts which compose it, and denounced them, one by one, in the most ample and unequivocal form.  In the English language we have the term *servant*, which we apply indiscriminately both to those held in voluntary subjection to another, and to those whose subjection is involuntary.  We have also the term *slave*, which is applicable exclusively to those held in involuntary subjection.  The Greek language had a word corresponding exactly in signification with our word servant; but it had none that answered precisely to our term slave.*  How then was an apostle, writing in Greek, to condemn *our slavery?*  Could it be done in the way in which some seem to think it must be done, before they will be convinced of its sinfulness?  How can we expect to find in Scripture the words 'slavery is sinful?' when the language in which it is written contained no term which expressed the meaning of our word slavery?  Would the advocates of slavery wish us to show that the apostles declare it to be unchristian to hold servants (douloi)?  This would have been denouncing, as criminal, practices far different from slaveholding.  But inspiration taught the holy penmen the only correct and efficacious method of conveying their condemnation of this unchristian system.  They pronounce of each one of those several things which constitute slavery, that it is sinful—thus clearly and forever denouncing the system, wherever it might appear, and whatever name it might assume.  If a writer should take up each part of our federal constitution separately and condemn it article by article, who would have the folly to assert that, after all, he had not expressly condemned the constitution?  Who would say that this thorough and entire disapproval of every part of the instrument of confederation must pass for nothing, and is no proof of the writer's hostility to it, because he has never said exactly in so many words, 'I disapprove of the Constitution of the United States?'  We see that he could condemn it most explicitly and thoroughly without even mentioning it by name.

 "Further, human language is so fluctuating that words often, in the lapse of time, change their meaning.  The word tyrant expresses now a very different idea from that which it once

* The words *oiketes, andrapodon,* are those which most nearly correspond, in the idea which they present, with our word slave.  But oiketes properly signifies a *domestic;* and andrapodon, *one taken and enslaved in war.*  The inspired writers could not have denounced *our sort of slavery,* by using either of these words.  If they had forbidden us to hold oiketai, they would have forbidden us the use of all domestics—if they had forbidden us to hold andrapoda, they might have been interpreted as forbidding our use only of *such slaves as have been taken and enslaved in war.*

conveyed. So the term Constitution of the United States, at some future period, from the alterations introduced into our government, may indicate something far different from that which it now indicates. It is true wisdom, then, when we wish to perpetuate our condemnation of a system or institution, to express our sentiments of the various *things* that constitute the system or institution, and not of the *mere name* by which it is now known. Thus our sentiments will be guarded from the misconceptions that may arise in the fluctuation of language. So that even if there were words in Greek, specifically set apart to designate the idea of slavery, inspiration would probably still have guided the apostles to their present form of expression in its condemnation. Had they used such language as this, 'slavery is sinful,' some modern apologists for the system might have alleged that our slavery was not such as existed among the Greeks—that slavery here was a different thing from that which the apostles denounced. But the course they pursued leaves no room for such a subterfuge. We have received the command, 'Love thy neighbor as thyself,' and we are conscious that we are violating the whole spirit as well as letter of this precept, when, for our own trifling pecuniary gain, we keep a whole race sunk in ignorance and pain. We are commanded to give our servants 'that which is just and equal,' and no sophistry can persuade us that we fulfil this towards those whom we deprive of the reward of their labor. We know that the idea of a bondman receiving a just and equal remuneration for his labor, never enters the minds of slaveholders. The precepts against fraud, oppression, pride, and cruelty, all cut directly through the heart of the slave system. Look back at the *constituents* and *the effects* of slavery, and ask yourself, 'Is not every one of these things directly at variance with the plainest commands of the gospel?' The maintenance of this system breaks not one law of the Lord, or two laws—it violates the whole code—it leaves scarcely one precept unbroken. And will any one, then, contend that slavery is not reprobated by God, and that he may participate in the system, and assist in its perpetuation, without deep criminality? Forbid it, conscience—forbid it, common sense! Gaming, horse-racing, gladiatorial shows in which men were hired to butcher each other, the selling of children by their parents, which was often practised in ancient days—all these things are condemned by the Scriptures, not by name, but (as slavery is condemned) by denouncing those crimes of which these acts are modifications and illustrations.

"These views of the sinfulness of slavery place it beyond all doubt, that it is the duty of every individual connected with the system to aid, vigorously and efficiently, in its abolition, and thus free himself from all participation in its criminality. How is this to be done? Certainly not by merely treating our slaves kindly, and thus mitigating the evils of their condition. You may say you have already, in the case of your own slaves, abolished the worst evils of the system, and that in every way you promote their comfort and welfare. Still duty absolutely requires at least one more step—a guarantee that their future happiness, and that of their children, shall not be at the mercy of another's caprice. And this can be effected only by a legal provision for their release from bondage. It is probable that the Romans were in a better condition under Titus than they would have been had they governed themselves. But the gentleness of his sway only aggravated the horrors of their situation, under his dark and bloody successors. Granting all that any man may urge in favor of his own kindness to his dependents, still he is, contrary to the laws of nature and of God, retaining them in a condition which is tolerable only under the most rare and favorable circumstances—which inevitably works woe and ruin, unless prevented by the singular virtue and generosity of an extraordinary master. Would we be willing that we and our children should be thus held? And remember that the fundamental principle of Christian morality is, that 'what things soever ye would that others should do unto you, do ye even so to them.' Are we complying with our Saviour's injunction, when we thus leave our fellow beings exposed to all the future miseries, which avarice, caprice, and cruelty may inflict? Yet we profess subjection to Christ's laws— 'He that knoweth my will and *doeth* it,' says the divine Redeemer, 'he it is that loveth me.' The very best condition of a slave for life is like the condition of those unfortunate men that we sometimes read of, who have been unjustly condemned to die—but mercy or policy arresting the execution of the sentence, they have, for a time, been permitted to go at large, yet liable every moment to be remanded to prison and to death. This is the situation of a slave, at his best estate—and who will say that either mercy or justice permits us to retain him in such a situation?

"It is often urged that our slaves are better off than our free negroes. If mankind had considered this plea for continuing to hold slaves a valid one, the whole world would have been still in slavery—for all nations have been at one time or other in some kind of slavery—and all despots urged this plea against their emancipation. Besides, no man ought to urge this as his reason for retaining his bondmen, unless he feels conscious that it is his real motive. And we willingly appeal to every man's conscience to say whether his own imagined interest is not his real motive for refusing to adopt any efficient measures for changing the condition of his servants. That our negroes, if emancipated, will be worse off, is, we feel, but the specious pretext for lulling our own pangs of conscience, and answering the argument of the philanthropist. None of us believe that God has so created a whole race, that it is better for them to remain in perpetual bondage. One mode of emancipation may be preferable to another—but any mode is preferable to the perpetuation, through generations to come, of a degrading bondage. History, with a hundred tongues, testifies that, as a general rule, to emancipate is to elevate. And it is vain for any man to argue against such a general law of nature by adducing the occasional departures, which have fallen under his own personal observation. We plant ourselves down on the broad and acknowledged principle, that God created all men capable of freedom—if, then, they have become unfit for this condition, it is by our fault they have become so; and our exertions, if we are willing to do our duty, can easily restore to them that fitness of which we have deprived them.

"As the conclusion of all that has been advanced, we assert it to be the unquestionable duty of every Christian, to use vigorous and immediate measures for the destruction of the whole system, and for the removal of all its unhappy effects. Both these objects should be contemplated in his efforts."